CHRONICLES of A SEER

CHRONICLES of A SEER

(THE PROPHECY)

Ramon Santos

© Copyright 2013—Ramon Santos
All rights reserved. This book is protected by the copyright laws of the United States of America. This book may not be copied or reprinted for commercial gain or profit. The use of short quotations or occasional page copying for personal or group study is permitted. Permission will be granted upon request. Unless otherwise identified, Scripture quotations are from the HOLY BIBLE, ENGLISH STANDARD VERSION© 2001 by Crossway Bibles, a publishing ministry of Good News Publishers. Used by permission. All rights reserved. Scripture quotations marked (NIV) are taken from the HOLY BIBLE, NEW INTERNATIONAL VERSION®. Copyright © 1973, 1978, 1984 by International Bible Society. Used by permission of Zondervan. All rights reserved. Scripture quotations marked (NASB) are taken from the HOLY BIBLE, THE NEW AMERICAN STANDARD BIBLE®. Copyright © 1960, 1962, 1963, 1968, 1971, 1972, 1973, 1975, 1977, 1995 by The Lockman Foundation, La Habra, CA. All rights reserved. Used by permission. (www.Lockman.org). Scripture quotations marked "MSG" are taken from The Message. Copyright 1993, 1994, 1994, 1996, 2000, 2001, 2002. Used by permission of NavPress Publishing Group, www.navpress.com. Scripture quotations marked (ASV) are taken from the AMERICAN STANDARD VERSION BIBLE. Public Domain.

ISBN: 1493783661
ISBN 13: 9781493783663
Library of Congress Control Number: 2013923213
CreateSpace Independent Publishing Platform
North Charleston, South Carolina

Published by:
FIRE ON THE MOUNTAIN
301 County Airport Road, Ste 208
Vacaville, CA 95688

www.iFireontheMountain.com

VENERATES AND ACKNOWLEDGEMENTS

FIRST, I SAY THANK YOU to my wife Lorrie. You are my truest friend, lover, and companion. You have held my hand and I yours in times of joy and laughter, in destitution, in wealth, and in victory. I also bow down with thanks to my children Jacob, Joshua, Josiah and our newest family member, Cara, our daughter in law, for the things they teach me.

To my family: I would especially like to acknowledge Grandfather Clement Stitt, Grandmother Fannie Witherspoon, Robinette Witherspoon, Adolph Witherspoon, Emanuel and Mary Witherspoon, Aunt Mary and Uncle Charlie Battle, all my cousins, and William (Bill) Kienzel. To my parents Raymond and Audrey Santos: thank you for loving us, pushing us to be better, and to go after our dreams. You taught me to go after what I want. Thanks to my sisters and their husbands, Anita and Mitch Celaya III and Tracy and Bob Vezer, who continue to inspire me. To my in-laws, Chris and George Roberts-Hague, I just want to say thank you for standing by us and encouraging us to grow in each other and in Christ. You are a testimony of God's love. Thanks to Aunt Dorothy Roberts, who in her nineties has welcomed and encouraged me. She speaks of God's grace continually, encouraging me in His journeys.

To those I call or have called mentors in times past, those who have helped to keep me on track: It is each one of you who have touched my life in ways that allowed me to grow and to share what has been given me. I say thank you to Dan McCollam,

Randy Clark, John Eldridge, John and Carol Arnott, *Toronto Airport Christian Fellowship Teams and Catch the Fire*, David and Deb Crone, *The Mission Teams*, Cleddie Keith, Ivan Tate, Bob Jones, Bill and Beni Johnson, Kris Vallotton, *Bethel Church Teams*, Rick Joyner, *The Morningstar Teams*, and Wayne and Diane LaCosse for believing in me. Thanks to all those who have imparted a piece of legacy into me and for the times we traveled together.

There are many other encouragers and intercessors I haven't room to name here. Nonetheless, I say thank you to you; you know who you are. Never stop encouraging. There are many others who need what you have, as I did.

And finally, many thanks to the teams that helped me in putting together the manuscripts of *SEERS in the KINGDOM (Their Stories)*, Carol C. and Cara Santos. Regarding this book, *CHRONICLES of A SEER*, I could not have done it without you Regina McCollam and Carol C. Thank you.

P.S. I ask the angelic hosts of heaven with the Holy Spirit to continue moving and releasing in you and through you the will of God and the desires of your heart. I pray this in Jesus' name. Amen.

CONTENTS

Venerates and Acknowledgements v
Preface ix
Introduction xi
Chapter 1   Grace, Hope, and Callings 1
Chapter 2   The Journey 13
Chapter 3   Dead Reckoning 19
Chapter 4   The Development 43
Chapter 5   Consequences with Favor 57
Chapter 6   The Return 75
Chapter 7   Get Ready 87
Chapter 8   Moravian Falls 95
Chapter 9   Epiphany 105
Chapter 10   Toronto, England & Paris 115
Chapter 11   The Awakening 125
Chapter 12   The Stadium 139
Chapter 13   Quickening 149
Chapter 14   A New Covering 165
Chapter 15   Stealing 177
Chapter 16   A Prophecy and Promise 193
   Teddy Roosevelt 205
Appendix I   Prophetic Terms and References 207

PREFACE

THESE ARE THE CHRONICLES of Ramon, a seer in a journey with supernatural and mystical encounters. These encounters, though unseen, affect the natural events of everyday life. There are stories throughout the Bible about those with abilities and gifts as stated in 1 Corinthians 12. These gifts seem to parallel the evolution of man in the appointed times of our evolution. These abilities seem to emerge with no scientific explanation, as they become uncanny in the release.

To relate these gifted endowments, I like to use scientific studies of the various light spectrums with dimensions of time and space. This comparison is a great analogy of many seer abilities.

There is a silent influence seers have on society and individuals that has been recorded over the centuries. It is time to tell the stories to open the minds of those who have no inclination about the unseen dimension and how it can and does affect all of us. In this particular journey of the telling, you will meet my Friend who guides me and teaches me how to walk in the gifts as a prophetic declaration that awaits its appointed time.

INTRODUCTION

WHAT IS A RO'EH? It is the Hebrew name for a seer. In today's terminology, it is one who receives numinous communication from a deity through visions or visual encounters. I will be using historical references from the Bible along with other scientific explanations throughout this narrative.

> *Seer:* Hebrew (ro-eh'); active participant of; a beholder in vision; or gazer; prophet: The basic lenses of communications are sight. To glimpse, notice, or observe events past present or future.
>
> To view; visit or attend as a spectator:
>
> To perceive by means of vision, trance, dreams.
>
> To scan or view, like electronic means: As a *satellite can see an entire country. (The far away approach)*
>
> Abilities: To perceive (things) with all senses; smell, taste, touch, hear, mental (awareness); discern; have spiritual; dimensional sight.
>
> *Objective:* Give attention or care to find out; make inquiry; To make sure or take care (of something) to *intercede.*

Jim Goll, a well-known author and seer, shares that there are three main components of a seer. Goll explains that distinguishing between a dream, vision, trance, or being translated is difficult at times. The reason it is difficult is because it is actually supernatural.

In biblical terms, you may literally be in the actual kingdom of God, which is His presence, known as the *Holy Spirit.*

Visions are the images released by the presence of God or the Holy Spirit in the form of a vision, trance, or dream.

Actual is the manifestation of the dreams, trances, or visions as God's presence is apparent in the manifestation. When God's presence shows up, there is always a manifestation in some way. It is like the light has been turned on in the dark.

I like using the word *ethereal,* which means the heavenly or celestial, when relating to the spiritual regions beyond the earth. These are the events I will be describing.

Hearing: The word prophet is used synonymously with the word seer throughout history. The word is used 23 times in the Old Testament, being first recorded in 1 Samuel 9:9. (Some of the prophets of that day were called seers.) The word prophet is first used in Genesis 20:7 and then another 233 times in Scripture. In many cultures, the name prophet is used as one who inquires of God or a deity mainly by hearing. This experience is known as a "*word of knowledge.*" This word is information that a person receives about something with no foreknowledge.

What the person receives can be from past, present, or future in visual, hearing, or combinations thereof. There are a few other names given to those who have and do get words in the mystical occult realms of religion. They are known as diviner, soothsayer, oracle, augur, and Chaldean. In today's scientific circles, premonition or physic are the words commonly used for receiving such supernatural information.

The Book of Daniel chapters 1 & 2 are good examples of seer ability and how it is used. In those chapters the king's counselors, which include the wise men, Chaldeans, sorcerers and diviners, are ordered to tell him what he dreamed and the meaning of his dream. The king also states that if they can-not tell him the dream and its meaning, he will kill all the counselors throughout his kingdom. Daniel hears of the proclamation and requests a meeting with the king. He informs the king that he will seek God about the dream and the interpretation. The rest of the story, which is found in the Book of Daniel, tells that the counselors were saved through Daniel's accurate interpretation.

I believe another Hebrew word embodies who a seer is, Emunah—it is more than belief and faith; it is who God says we are and who we are to be as we come into agreement with HIS Word.[1]

---

1 Luke 1:38 "Let it be so as you have spoken" to the Angel of the *Lord*.

Chapter One

GRACE, HOPE, AND CALLINGS

PURSUANT TO CIRCUMSTANCES IN one's life, events transpire to help prepare individuals. As I reflect back on the events that occurred over the decades of my life, one in particular stands out, as it will affect a nation of billions.

I was looking as my eyes opened on a clear sunny day into the spiritual realm with distinct visibility. I was intrigued as I observed. The blade struck, penetrating deep into the ground. I saw it going through what looked to be an outline of a massive, dark image of an angel lying face down as if asleep. It was completely black though in dimensional degrees of blackness. The point struck through what looked like the angel's left shoulder blade, through the huge wing protruding from it, through where the heart would be, and protruding back out of the front of his body, fastening him to the ground. There was a flash as my vision shifted back into the natural reality from that realm. I heard a screeching scream of agonizing pain, and then, it ended instantly.

As the scream ended, the ground oscillated. This action manifested as a tremor. Viewing the surroundings in the distance, I saw the buildings ever so slightly sway back and forth as lights came on in most of them while the earthquake rippled through the distant hills of the region.

The hidden weapons of God's love are coinciding with technological growth as God is releasing His knowledge, wisdom, power, and love supernaturally and scientifically. This, I hope you will see as I take you on this poignant epiphany of a Seer.

As a seer, I have come to realize that the evolving of science has many similarities to that which is gifted to the prophetic realm. I would like to touch a little on this to open our minds to the powers of life found in the physics of light spectrums, dimensions, and sound echelons. In the electromagnetic energy of light come levels of radioactive power. In the basic light realms, power is released in each light spectrum. The typical person in the natural is limited in the ranges of these spectrums to the visible colors of light.

Some of these light spectrums include infrared, ultraviolet, gamma rays, and x-rays. It was a vision/dream given to Marie Curie that opened the doors to electromagnetic energy to which she gave the name "*radiation.*" The enhancement of technology since her time has expanded her discovery to include telecommunication, photography, T-Ray imaging, guidance systems, heating, the expanded use of electricity, lasers, note *photobiomodulation* (healings) of nervous systems, herpes virus, and other diseases. Other uses are the gas and electric companies' use of infrared as an aid in the pre-emptive actions of potential disasters.

What I see is a similarity to the *actual* presence of another gift given to man. These tools will show potential hot spots which cannot be seen with the natural eye. This is very similar to the way a seer sees or hears. The seer can then intercede by communication with God, tapping into the Lord's desire to stop an ill-fated occurrence from happening. In the hearing realm, the dominant radio band is C for the average person. Seers and hearers are hard-wired by God in these different levels from sight, sound, dimensions, and time. It was Albert Einstein, one of the greatest minds of our time, who addressed these in his scientific details from $E=MC2$ and his Theory of Relativity. Think about how a blind person hears things that the normal person does not. A blind person will push to exercise his or her other senses and learn to attune to the other spheres of communication.

Each sphere (sight, sound, touch) has a magnitude of viable power that comes with it. When I look at the electromagnetic energy harnessed by man in the light spectrums and compare them to what happens in the *actual* encounters, it is very similar. The greatest difference I find is the actual encounters (Kingdom presence of the *Holy Spirit*) bring greater power with no harm—pureness of health in all aspects to life with a craving for even more.

Let's review the spheres of electromagnetic energy:

Alpha: a low penetrating power.

Beta: a negative force, a little more powerful in penetrating through barriers.

Gamma: a greater energy with power as used with (X-ray, Pulsars, Quasars, radio galaxies, and lasers which have some of the highest frequencies and power).

The gamma sphere reminds me of what I see at times coming from people. When looking at people as they extend their hand openly in prayer, I have observed rays of light coming out in the direction they point their hand. At other times I have seen beams of light like lasers penetrating into the person/people. This brought my thoughts to *What*, *When*, and *Why* this is happening in the supernatural? Looking into the science of quantum physics, I discovered the following.

Light from a laser is often tightly focused and does not diverge much, resulting in the traditional laser beam. In simplest terms, light is used to stimulate the electrons into a certain state known as "optical pumping." When the electrons collapse into a lower-energy unexcited state as they become photons, let's encase them between mirrors with nowhere to go. Then as they amplify, increasing in energy (electrons), they need to expand into a higher level. By putting a small opening or a hole in the mirror, the light is allowed to escape, and you now have a laser beam. In other words, energy is being caught, built up, and released. In the principles of quantum mechanics, when you use a laser to create a beam of light where all of the photons are in a coherent state (non-energizing), if they are out of sync (not in agreement) not in step together, there will be no laser beam. Likewise, we usually should be in agreement with God's will for the presence to flow through us. Being in sync with Holy Spirit and God through Christ is not a statement of fact but free will of choice. In the *actual* encounters, this principle works the same whenever we come into agreement with the kingdom of Heaven.

The actual encounter brings power that enters us—the vessel magnifying in us—beyond our abilities to handle at that time. Then as we lay hands, point, or direct it by our speech in agreement, that power is released like a laser beam. It is God's Holy Spirit expanding through us—if we are willing.

Not only is authority unbounded, but the power generated also has no bounds, for the kingdom of God is limitless. We, like a rifleman, must learn to handle the recoil when the power is released through the shooting.

The *actual* presence in a seer's sight has a manifestation from the power released by the vision, just as the recoil does. It is a known fact that when one is communicating with God through the Holy Spirit, that *actual* power is released through the communication. It is known to bring forth *healings, words of knowledge, signs, miracles, and wonders.* This is similar to electromagnetic energy. I believe this is why it is hard for anyone who is receiving from God to distinguish between the types of *actual* revelation from the *Holy Spirit.* The question is: Which are known as the manifestations of the Holy Spirit?

It is not by might nor by power but by my Spirit says the LORD. (Zechariah 4:6)

A teaching done by Dan McCollam uses the theory of quantum physics. He has done scientific tests and brought in scholars' research to teach on the power of sound using the visual dimensional attributes to prove how positive sound creates and negative sound destroys, just as with the pureness of light and darkness.

God is pure truth and light, and we now have access to God without the penalty of death, as would have happened in the time of Moses.[2] Because of the coming and intervention of Christ Jesus, we now have access to the gifts Paul speaks of in 1 Corinthians 12.[3] I have included pages at the end of the book for you to write down what Holy Spirit gives to you as you read these revelations.

There is one fact that is certain with a seer: what they have seen has happened, is happening, or will happen. A seer has the ability to intercede in some way, as you will see in the encounters I will share in this book. The mystery is in the timing of when the event will unfold. Think of a triathlon athlete who can run, swim, and bicycle great distances as he or she is covering three totally different physical events to triumph for the goal— the athlete is always training for each. The prophetic gifts have a great ability to help save, alter, or improve life, but like a triathlon athlete, a seer is covering many events. Remember, though, that when a gift is in operation, it must actually be released to affect a circumstance. For instance, when the word of knowledge is given and not released, it is nothing more than a dream or vision. The *"word of knowledge"* has to be spoken to be released as a prophetic word in order to change a circumstance.

---

[2] Exodus 3

[3] Now there are varieties of gifts, but the same Spirit; and there are varieties of service, but the same Lord; and there are varieties of activities, but it is the same God who empowers them all in everyone. To each is given the manifestation of the Spirit for the *common good.*

Following is one of many documented lessons derived from American history through a prophetic person who I believe was a seer.

JUST BEGUN TO FIGHT
In the last century, there was a military officer named Colonel Billy Mitchell of the United States Army Air Division. It was in the early 1920's, and Billy was predicting that the U.S. needed a separate division of the military, an Air Corp for what was going to happen in the Pacific during the years to come. He predicted this in 1918. The years continued to pass as he pursued Congress and those of greater authority for another military division. In 1926, Billy Mitchell, now a General, received a premonition and predicted that Japan would initiate war in the Pacific against the U.S. with an aerial attack. This vision thrust the General into fully pushing to establish an Air Corp. The U.S. Congress then ordered General Mitchell to "stand down" from pushing the issue of creating the US Air Corp. In 1928, however, Billy again states, *"Japan never declares war before attacking."* As he spoke this word of revelation in 1932, he was declaring that the Japanese would bomb Hawaii.

You cannot quiet down a man who gets a revelation when he knows it will come to pass. After some time, Congress, having failed to quiet him down on this issue, had General Mitchell demoted. They hoped that he would retire after the humiliation.

The boldness of General Mitchell caused me to think of Peter and John as they stood in front of the rulers of the people and were ordered not to speak.

But Peter and John replied to them, "Whether it is right in the sight of God to listen to you and obey you rather than God, you must decide (judge). But we [ourselves] cannot help telling what we have seen and heard. (Acts 4:19-20)

Grace, Hope, and Callings

General Mitchell looked at those who demoted him and stated, "I have just begun to fight." He was later court-martialed by political bureaucracy because he followed the vision, prophecy, premonition, or word of knowledge that he was given. Here Mitchell followed with all his heart the ability that is embedded in each of us known as *emunah*.[4] This credence develops in a seer through time from the legitimacy of the revelations.

This was not a man who had gone fanatical. In fact, General Mitchell had a track record of foreseeing and achieving what needed to be done as his high-ranking military status proved. He was dedicated to God and country and would not compromise, as can be read in his biography. General Billy Mitchell died in 1936 having never seen the revelation of the vision come to its completion.

The Japanese did bomb Hawaii in 1946 and then declared war on the U.S. as history has recorded. It was just as General Billy Mitchell had foreseen, and from this, the military Air Corp was established. The attack was so great, it caused a separation of this Air Corp unit from the U.S. Army, and it became the United States Air Force. The biography of General Mitchell is now required reading at the United States Air Force Officers Academy.

It was General Mitchell's destiny to bring forth this revelation and to release it into the proper channels as it awaited its time. He had used this gift to declare the unseen works to come. General Mitchell's sight into the mystical dimensions of the future shows how one person can make a difference. The importance of preparation and trusting in God's Word, the need to hear God and act, can be seen within the lines of General Mitchel's legacy. Mitchell would not shake the dust from his feet when declaring the word he was given.

You see, no matter what is given, it is always our choice to listen or not, to do or not just as we saw illustrated through the

---

4 A Hebrew word for more than belief and faith.

choices Congress and the bureaucrats of General Mitchell's day made. This is only one event in history, out of the hundreds that are recorded, where prophecy or premonitions were at work to awaken the people to what was about to happen.

There are trials and circumstances of everyday life that can and do change the heart of the seer, which will in turn affect how we deliver the knowledge we receive. There are also some who have misused this prophetic ability for exploiting, manipulating, and or self-gain throughout history. Numbers chapter 22 records how Balaam had a confrontation with an Angel of the LORD because of the misuse of the gift. He was given a choice to refrain and correct.

First of all, the gifts are not to be used for manipulating or for self-gain; they are given for improving, encouraging, and helping to build with virtue. Here are a few simple guidelines that I have learned.

1. When you release what is given, release just what is given; do not add or take away.
2. Do not let your personal dealings or issues intertwine into the release that you are giving. (Don't let anything personal have a foothold on what you release.)
3. Confirm what you are getting. Does it edify and encourage? Look to see and hear the reactions of what you are saying—especially in different cultures.

Now if what a seer sees is something that tears down the receiving person, then they should speak the opposite of what is seen or heard. Examples:

Negative	**Opposite**
Stabbing in the back	Supportive, Got your back
Liar	Honest, Truism
Debauchery	Benevolence, Unselfishness
Death	Life, protection

The reason the seer releases the opposite is that as the person receiving the word hears, he also can declare and proclaim this positive trait over his life effectively overcoming the current negative behavior. When a seer speaks, it is like a small ship rudder that sets the direction for the ship, creating a new hope and a door of opportunity.

Just as the Declaration of Independence was written for the United States of America with the Constitution to keep us in check from corruption in all forms, so the *Holy Spirit* checks our hearts continually to see that we are not hardening our hearts or being corrupted from the outside sources of life.

When a seer sees negative or bad, they must continue to look past what they see, for there is much more. Don't be overanxious to delivery part of a vision and miss the rest that is still to come, as impatience may cause unnecessary problems. The story in Daniel chapter 10 is a good example of continuing to look beyond what is seen initially. The *"Vision of the Four Beasts"* changed to *"The Ancient of Days"* to conclude with *"The Son of Man"* who conquered with life, protection, and goodness, as in this story.

STARBUCKS

Standing in line one day to buy a drink at the local Starbucks, I overheard a conversation going on in front of me between two people. The person standing in front was talking about dropping out of college, presenting all kinds of reasons to the other person. As they continued conversing, I was translated into a God-given vision about that person's future. When I returned from the vision, I jumped into the conversation, speaking right into what was shown to me: *"The Lord showed me this single young man a little older with a family."*

Then suddenly, I was translated into a vision again as time jumped ahead while they continued speaking, *"I watched his achievements resulting from staying in college as he and his family affected the lives of others."* Then I heard, *"If he doesn't finish college, he would still be doing the same things that he is doing now, making excuses, being in the same position, wishing that he had finished school."* I released the revelation to him with a blessing in the name of the Jesus. The Holy Spirit was not done with me, however. As the Presence lit me up like the watts of a three-way bulb, I jumped up from the increase of power.

The *Actual* encounter of the Spirit was present with power and authority. It had me slurring my words as though intoxicated. Now at the front of the line, it was time to order my drink from the barista. I noticed she had a brace on her wrist. "What happened?" I asked her. She told me it was carpel tunnel and that she was going into surgery the next week to have it fixed. I was feeling the increased nudging of the presence of Holy Spirit as He was igniting the atmosphere.

I said, "Okay, Lord," and I then asked the barista if I could pray for her wrist to be healed. "Yes," she responded. I rebuked the pain and commanded complete healing into the arm, tendons, and muscles, rebuking all other aliments in the name of Jesus. Pausing then, I asked her how it felt. As she took off the brace and moved the wrist around, she told me that it felt much better; the pain was completely gone.

"Just to play it safe," she said as she slipped the brace back on. I declared that her wrist is healed, and we thanked Jesus! A couple weeks later, I saw her again, and she told me that no surgery was needed! Thank you, Jesus.

He sent them out to proclaim the kingdom of God and to heal.[5]

This is what happens at an *Actual* encounter with the Kingdom at hand as the Holy Spirit works through you.

Going back to the vision of the young man, it was over five years later that I saw the young man with his family. He finished college

---
5 Luke 9:2

Grace, Hope, and Callings

with a new career, accomplishing his dreams, and was now helping others. I saw him also as one who brings both the community and church together.

This is a legacy you can leave for your children that will live on.

There are seers who use their ability in serving deities in occult practices. These are known as diviners, palm readers, etc. These people open doors into dimensional realms of unclean spirits, and it comes with a cost. The unclean entity may abstract its *payment then or later, from them or their descendants, depending on the cost for their services.* I have seen the cost associated with unclean spirits ranging from simple ailments, to diseases, cancers, or even the person's soul and life. There is only one thing that can cancel debts to deities or evil spirits, and that is the blood of *Christ*.

In the testimonies to follow, you will see how children and adults have conquered ties with unclean spirits through the blood of *Christ*.

There is one authority who has the power to cancel debts owed to unclean spirits and remove any other sins of life: *Christ Jesus*. There is one requirement to having those debts cancelled: believe in Jesus Christ as the Son of God,[6] and ask Him to forgive you of your sins. Then ask Him to come into your life and accept Him as your Lord and Savior. When you open this door, it touches your *soul, mind, spirit, and body,* setting you free, as your past is stricken from the records—yours and God's. You are now a new person in *Christ*.

If you do not know *Jesus Christ* the Son of God or do not have a relationship with Him, I would like to stop and pray this prayer with you right now.

---

6 John 3:16-17 For God so loved the world, that he gave his only Son, that whoever believes in him should not perish but have eternal life. For God did not send his Son into the world to condemn the world, but in order that the world might be saved through him.

Jesus Christ, you are the Son of God, and I ask You to forgive me of my sins, and to come into my life and into me. I want to build a relationship with You as my Savior. I accept You as my Lord and King. I ask the Holy Spirit to come fill me with all that You have for me, in Your name Jesus, Amen.

Chapter Two

THE JOURNEY

IN THE 1950'S THEATRICAL, "Harvey," there is a six-foot rabbit that only Elwood (played by Jimmy Stewart) could see. This visual lamp post has stayed with me since childhood. It helped me to understand as I saw supernatural things, that there are those who can see in the spiritual dimensions what others cannot see. The Holy Spirit—which I did not understand then—is the third Person of the Trinity—Father, Son, and Holy Spirit—all God. This I knew to be true without question from what I saw, but others who could not see what I saw had different perceptions. I tried to find ways to communicate what I saw, but I made little headway. To me, the Holy Spirit was like Harvey, a friend who helps and guides you with only your best interest at heart.

This understanding was especially needful as I was growing into adulthood. There were certain people who would criticize my gift of spiritual sight as being from the devil. The common argument they sited was that the gifts as recorded in 1 Corinthians 12 no longer exist and that these gifts were only used in the past as a sign to the unbelieving.

As I pondered their arguments, I considered the beginning chapters of both the Old and New Testaments: Genesis chapter 1 and John chapter 1. The first chapter of Genesis says:

The Spirit of God was hovering over the waters. (vs. 2 NIV)

The Hebrew word translated Spirit is *rûah*, which means "the extension of…" (also, "breath, mind, and or Spirit"). In verses 3, 6, 8, 9, 11, 20, 26, the Scripture says, "GOD said…" in Hebrew, the word for "said" is *âmar*, which means "to declare." Further on in Genesis chapter one, verse 26, it says, **"Let us make man in our** own image after our likeness." Putting these Scriptures together brings further revelation to the question of whether the gifts of the Spirit are still operating today since we are made in God's image and the gifts are of His natural makeup.

The Apostle John brings the beginning of Genesis together in a stunning declaration that sets this natural makeup in gold and platinum:

In the beginning was the Word (Christ), and the Word was with God, and the Word was God. He was in the beginning with God. All things were made through him, and without him was not anything made that was made. In him was life and the life was the light of men. (John 1:1-4, parenthesis mine)

Consider, also, John 17:5.

And now, Father, glorify me in your own presence with the glory that I had with you before the world existed. (John 17:5)

As I meditated on these sections of Scripture, I realized I now had an explanation of the Trinity for those who could not see. These spirit gifts are actually in our genetic makeup, as we are created after God's likeness.[7] God is the same yesterday, today, and forever, therefore, mankind is still evolving into their completeness.[8]

Remember this: God creates; the devil duplicates.

The book of Acts speaks of seers:

God declares, that I will pour out my Spirit on all flesh, and your sons and your daughters shall prophesy, and that they shall see visions, and dream dreams. The male servants and female servants shall prophesy. (Acts 2:17-18)

---

7   Genesis 1:26
8   Hebrew 13:8

As I was writing this morning, I was reminded of an important conversation I had that illustrates this. The severely cracked windshield of my SUV was being replaced. The insurance company sent the new windshield to my residence with an installer. When Jorge finished installing my new windshield, I invited him to come into my home office in order to conclude the paperwork for the repair. Jorge saw my Bible sitting on my desk. "Are you a Christian?" he asked, a bit hesitant.

"Yes, I am!"

Feeling confident that I would understand him, Jorge began to tell me about his encounters with God. He had not known Jesus Christ very long as his Savior, only a few years. He had been hearing stories about Christ the Healer, and Jorge's interest to know Jesus more had been piqued. In our conversation, Jorge told me that He actually asked the Lord if the healing stories he had heard were true. The Lord then said to Jorge as he was getting ready to go to a Shawn Smith concert, "Take your inhaler with you." He explained to me that he has a severe case of asthma.

It was during this concert that Jesus answered Jorge's questioning about healing. He showed up healing many that night. Jorge himself was overwhelmed by the power of the Holy Spirit—just as he had been on the day he gave his life to the Lord.

"Jesus healed me of asthma," he tells me, "'and it has been two years now since I was healed!" Ignited with more passion, he told me other testimonies of what the Lord is now doing through him. He also shared how God is healing wounds he received from Christians who do not believe that God still heals people today. Their doubts caused him to begin to question the abilities and gifts God had given him, and he was even contemplating giving up the supernatural ministry of healings, signs, miracles, and wonders.

"I know what happened to me, so how can others says it is not so?" Jorge questioned. We talked more, and by sharing a few testimonies of what I have seen Jesus do and what the Holy Spirit has done through me, I encouraged him to continue to partner with the Holy Spirit in the supernatural

I realized, as I talked to Jorge, how important it is that people not inflict their own doubts onto someone else, even if their own flame has been extinguished. Instead, take every opportunity to reignite the torch again by receiving sparks from a person who carries the flames of God's passion, like Jorge.

If you do not want be ignited again (perhaps life has torn you down and you are in a deep place of discouragement), then I respectfully suggest that you move out of the way by saying nothing negative to discourage another; consider blessing them in their accomplishments.

I would like to pray for you now:

Lord, I ask send the Holy Spirit to reignite the flame and transform the minds of those who are lost or misguided. Amen.

I know the disabled people who were healed when Jorge prayed for them were certainly glad that he did not listen to those doubters. My point is that these encounters and spiritual gifts *do* exist in our day—they are not just a part of our past church history. To have them activated in your life, all you have to do is ask Jesus said,

> *Very truly I tell you, whoever believes in me will do the works I have been doing, and they will do even greater things than these, because I am going to the Father. And I will do whatever you ask in my name, so that the Father may be glorified in the Son. (John 14:12-13 NIV)*

I find myself moving forward on this from the above verse. It speaks of Jesus as
1) *The way,*
2) *The truth,*
3) *The life,*
4) *The authority.*

And then tells us the power has been given to us to fully preach the Truth which is Jesus as the light of the world.

Ignorance can darken our ability to grow in life and love, and staying in a false mindset releases a virus that can hurt and cripple us in many ways. These particular "viruses" need to end, just as prejudices needed to end with the abolishment of slavery in the USA over a century ago. These viruses can mutate, linger around, and continue to cause harm, just like chronic infections or like keloid skin that forms over an infected wound during the healing process. The cure and the truth are in the Scriptures being fulfilled in the love of the Father through us.

I recommend that you take five minutes before starting each day and ask the Holy Spirit to open your mind, revealing God's love and truth. As you do this, you will begin to experience more encounters with God as your mind and heart become ablaze with the fire of life.

I know this was a heavenly appointment for Jorge and me. We prayed together seeking more knowledge and wisdom from God to move with authority and power released from the Heavenly Kingdom. We both were strengthened and sharpened in our relationship with Christ.

Remember this: when you believe you have mastered something, beware! You could actually miss the bigger revelation. I don't want to be one who ignores in the Scriptures the things I don't agree with just to substantiate my own conclusions. In order to make this a better world, we must transform our Western way of learning and thinking to come into alignment with the Scriptures the way God intended them. We will often find that we share varying opinions with people on biblical points, but our love for one another should be greater than our individual opinions.

TRANSFORMATION

Now let's continue on into the excursions of seers moving through space, time, and dimensions, as they are one and the same. They can be measured together or independently in the state of motion.

Simply said, seers are watching events pass by before or after they happen. They are independent of the events, unless they have been translated into the event itself. The latter is known as "Euclidean space perception."

These dimensions of time and space seen through a seer have been called "mystical" throughout history. The journey brings encounters with testimonies of Christ as the love of the Father is shown to us.

Now we will hear my story, starting from the beginning so as to not miss keys that are given as we trek.

Let's begin with my culture and background.

Chapter Three

DEAD RECKONING

MY DAD RAYMOND, OF Republic of Cabo Verde heritage, was the youngest of 22 children, five of whom were born in the USA. He has abilities which he never speaks about. His own father died when he was only two years old, and his mother died when he was twelve years old. Now orphaned, he was raised by his oldest sister, my Aunt Mary.

In his teens, my dad joined the military, becoming a career man in the United States Air Force. There he met my mother Audrey. When I was born, I was given the name "Ramon," which quickly got shortened to "Baby Ray." Family and friends eagerly awaited my arrival, especially Bryan and Ruby Samuels. The Samuels were a mixed marriage couple, as Ruby was Japanese.

During this time of history, prejudice was openly expressed in the USA. My Dad and Bryan both tried to keep the racial issues of the world away from their families. The two of them were stationed together at the same military bases over the next two decades.

My father, Raymond, received transfer orders to another air base. Before leaving, we moved into a temporary base housing block that was comprised of fully furnished duplexes. The buildings were divided by a sidewalk with a sandbox in front. Here, a divine mark was left on me as a small child not even old enough to go to pre-school. This occurrence led me to make a vow to God in my youth in which I swore that I would never let it happen to anyone else.

A little girl and I were playing with toys in the sandbox located between the duplex units. One of the toys was a little ship. Suddenly, the little girl's mother came out the door yelling at her daughter because she was playing with me.

"You do not play with them niggers!" Grabbing the child, the little girl's mother quickly took her inside their house. I ran into my house straight into the arms of my mother, crying at the confusion and cruelty I felt in the atmosphere, though I had no understanding of what just happened. My mom gently picked me up, hugging me as she tried to calm me down. "Honey, that lady is sick with an illness, and she needs help."

After a while, my mother put me down saying, "Now go back outside and play..." Looking into her face, a tear ran down her cheek. This was a moment in time for me—not forgotten—a charting point in my life with each decade that followed.

Eventually, we transferred to the Philippines. It was there that I began to experience strange, unnatural things in the physical.

One day, I was playing outside with some friends racing our bicycles down a gravel road in the housing area just off base when a very bizarre thing happened to me. All I recall is suddenly waking up propped up onto a crutch and standing against the shower wall of my house. I had been found on the side of a road lying in the ditch which doubled as the sewer system.

This was the first incident of this kind that I experienced, but certainly not the last. Similar things happened to me a few more times. One time I woke up in my bed with people standing over me. On another occasion, I went flying into the ditch again, though neither my parents nor the kids I was playing with had any idea of what had happened.

I don't remember what led up to this next event; was it from these reoccurring occurrences? I don't actually know.

It was during this time that I decided to run away from home.

DISCERNING THE VOICE

It was a very early morning, not long after one of these bizarre occurrences, that I heard this eerie unsettling voice (later in life I realized it was unclean whatever it was), "Nobody loves you...they don't care about you…just go…leave, run away!" Throughout the night I kept hearing this voice repeating that no one loved me. The sunlight had not pierced the darkness of night yet.

I got up out of my bed as I continued listening to the words of that eerie voice, walked out the backdoor of the house, and left home. I began walking along the side of my house to head out of the front gate. Then, suddenly, out of nowhere, I heard another Voice loudly in the air. Looking all around me, I realized that there was nobody there, so, I continued walking towards the front gate. Then I heard this second Voice speak to me again, "Where will you go?" it asked.

I paused, thinking about what I had just heard, all the while looking around to see who was speaking to me. I didn't find the source of this new voice and decided to obey the sound of the first voice to leave home anyway.

As I continued walking, the Voice spoke yet again, "What will you eat?"

I stopped in my tracks, looking all around me and wondering what was going on and who it was that was speaking to me! Slowly, I took a couple more steps towards the front gate. That same Voice spoke again in a euphonious tone, "Where will you live?"

Exasperated I cried out, "Who cares?"

But the response of the Voice this time was a tone unfamiliar to me and very much unexpected, "They love you… yes, they love you. Your parents love you."

I began to cry uncontrollably as I was overwhelmed with a rush of emotions shooting through me. I don't know how long I stood there…but eventually, the sun began to break through the night. After the longest time, I wiped away my tears.

"I am going back home…I don't care if I get in trouble," I told myself. Punishment for attempting to run away from home didn't matter to me in that moment; it was the words I had heard—with that Voice!—that meant so much to me. I spun around and headed to the back door of my house.

As I reached for the door handle, I realized it was locked! I stood there a moment trying to decide what to do. I started knocking on the back door, and my dad answered. Boy was he surprised! (I could tell by the sound of his voice which rose from shock to anger.) Still, I was relieved to be back inside the house…I was home.

My dad, however, stood there looking at me, very puzzled, and I could see his anger level rising.

"What were you doing outside? You are supposed to be in bed!" he shouted. I just stood there looking at him. I had no answers to give him.

"What were you doing out there?" He asked me again. I knew I was in big trouble now, so I lied.

"Uh, I thought I heard something outside…" I knew right away that was the wrong answer.

The echo in Dad's voice signaled that I was in big trouble, "You don't open that door! You don't go outside! Do you hear me? I said, do you hear me?"

Shaking my head up and down, a smile began to form as I continued to hear that voice with the sweet words rippling through my thoughts, "They love you…your parents love you!" Looking my dad in the face, I tried to hide my smile because I knew he would misunderstand why I was smiling. I knew what was coming next when I saw my dad grab his belt… I stood there waiting.

Even before the spanking, tears were falling down my face as I heard that love in the voice…and the smile never left me. The love I felt from those words was absolutely overwhelming. I felt no pain from the wallops of my dad's belt, no matter how many times I got struck. All that mattered in that moment was knowing that my parents loved me.

A verse in 1 John describes this love:

God is love, and whoever abides in love abides in God, and God abides in him. (1John 4:16)

I actually didn't realize until adulthood that it was because of God's presence on me that I felt no pain during my spanking.

The Voice that I experienced that day became a lighthouse; it helped me to distinguish between different voices I was hearing, one meant for good the others for suffering. Jesus said:

I have other sheep that are not of this fold. I must bring them also, and they will listen to my voice. (John 10:16)

The bizarre, physical, mystical episodes I had been having diminished to almost nil after that encounter. Our two years in the Philippines went quickly, and our family would be leaving the country with Anita, another new baby sister. My dad and Uncle Bryan had received orders to go to the combat zone of Vietnam, and the rest of the family moved stateside to an Air Force base in Salina, Kansas.

The transition to a new school brought new adventures for me. One day, some of the class decided to stay in from recess to talk and have fun. Along with our teacher, we kids were discussing life and talking about what we wanted to be and do when we got older. One girl brought up the subject of finding a husband and asked the question, "How do you pick one?" Our teacher responded with, "You pick ten specific things that you want in a husband or wife and you do not budge on them no matter what! The rest of the specific things you do or do not want in your spouse or relationship that are more than ten items on your list you are to give and take together." Marriage is a two-sided relationship, and growing to become a better person is done together.

That really made an impression on me as I meditated on what the teacher said. I began to write my own list, putting it to memory. This was the start of my basic list—my measuring stick—for a girlfriend, and eventually, my wife.

- No liars
- No drunks

- No druggies
- No cheaters
- Truthful

Later that morning, I prayed to God about what was on my heart. I knew I had no control over life's outcomes, but God did. I knew that all I had to do was ask, and I knew He would do what I asked. Jesus is always true to what He said He would do because that's who He is. I knew this as a child because I always held onto truth. In Hebrew, the word for "truth and belief together" is *emunah*. Jesus said:

> *Whatever you ask in my name, this I will do, that the Father may be glorified in the Son.14 If you ask me* anything in my name, I will do it. (John 14:13-14)*

In my prayers to the Lord as a child, I held these things in my heart and mind, knowing that no matter what, God is One who holds to His promises. He is true to His promises. Truth is who He is. In the years to come, you, too, will see promises and desires of your heart come into fulfillment because He is true to His Word.

CHILDS PRAYER

I was the last child with the Santos name, so I asked God, "Can I have a son to carry on the family name?" Then quickly I said "No…two sons would be better." Then, as I paused, I wondered, "What if something happens to my sons?" So I prayed, "Lord, no…I mean, three sons would be the best."

Then I asked, "God, if I could raise my family before You, have me do the things You want me to do."

I concluded my prayer by asking God one final request: "I do not want any kids except from the girl I am supposed to marry…I don't want to pick the wrong girl." I was a child…at that time, I knew nothing about how kids were made. I was careful to end my prayer with, "Please!" These were promises I expected from God.

I also learned from experience as an adult that you can prophesy into your own destiny as well as bring a curse upon yourself without realizing it. Peter did this in Matthew 26:74 after he denied Jesus three times on the night of His trial.

It was during these years that my dreaming at night began to take on a different nature. In much the same way that I had to learn to distinguish between the two different voices I was hearing when I ran away from home, so too, I had to learn the types of eccentric dreams I was having and their representative significance. One dream in particular kept repeating itself in my youth and then again at different times throughout my life. I began to learn how to evaluate my dreams much the same way I would approach problem solving puzzles or equations. As I took a teaching post later as an adult, problem-solving became much more a part of the way I lived my life.

BLACK LIMO CAR DRIVER AND THE VOICE

These eccentric dreams with their deviations came with the same unique intention to entice, to capture, and to control by temptation. They would often begin with me playing or walking somewhere as a child or a youth, when suddenly, out of nowhere, a big, black car that looked like a four-door limousine would pull up alongside of me. The driver was a figure of a man that had no recognizable facial features—just the outlined blackness as deep as a bottomless well. As I stood there viewing the nice car and observing the driver who also seemed nice, he would ask me, "Do you need a ride?" or "Would you like to go for a ride?" I sensed the sound of his voice, however, was coming from a very dark source. Yet, I always responded to his invitation with, "Okay."

The big, dark, shadow-figure of a driver would get out of the car and open the passenger door for me. He drove us around for a little while; that's when things started to feel strange to me. Looking at the driver, I would say, "Please let me out...!" But the driver ignored my request. So, I tried to open the car door, but the latch would not work. Moving to the other door I would discover that it's latch was also jammed. Then I began to try to roll down the car windows, but they too wouldn't open.

Suddenly I would hear that Voice I knew so well saying to me, "Kick out the bottom of the floor hard under your feet." With that instruction, I began to stomp the floor of the car with all of my might. The panel finally would give way, allowing me to escape out of the floor of the car.

This reoccurring dream never happened the same way twice. Each time, the circumstance of how I got into the car was different. The car was always the same deep black but different in shape and shades of black. Each time I would get into the back seat to go for a ride with the driver, and each time, he would not pull over. I always felt trapped in the car. The driver would always apologize, giving some reason why he could not stop the car to let me out. Each time I forgave him. In one version of the dream, I heard the Voice say, "Kick out the window." So I kicked the window, and it started wobbling back and forth. I heard, "Kick it again!" So I laid back in the rear seat and with both legs began double kicking the window. The window went flying out of the door, and I jumped out of the car door window, running all the way home.

Years passed before this dream reappeared again. In this case, the driver pulled up in a big, black sports car asking me if I would like to drive the car. My eyes widen at the thought: *If I am driving the car, then I can go where I want and get out whenever I want!* Responding, "Yes!" to the driver, I bent over to look at the dash board of the car. As I climbed into this sports car, however, the dark shadow of a man pushed me into the passenger seat of the car. Then the driver got into the driver's seat and immediately locked the doors, speeding off down the street.

I demanded the driver stop the car, but he only responded, "No." Planning my escape, I remembered all the previous times when I had kicked out windows or stomped on the floor panels I tried each of these tactics but nothing happened. Again, I felt trapped.

I said to myself, "What haven't I tried?" So I kicked the door itself with all that was in me, and with that, the door flew off the car as the car was moving. I realized in that moment that in order to defeat an enemy, you have to consider different possibilities, continually initiating new ideas and ways to overcome your impossible situation. From my dreams, I learned that when God is engaged with our lives, He never uses the same patterns or techniques. While the driver used different circumstances to entice, control, and capture me, the Voice showed me how to escape each time from the car in different circumstances. The driver was never successful in his attempts, however. I knew that God was teaching me His ways through these dream experiences. He gave me a mind to think and reason. He was teaching me and maturing me in my friendship with Him.

FAMILY

That year went fast. My dad received orders to go a new air base in Japan, and the family stopped en route to visit relatives in Chicago and Boston before heading to the Orient.

There were others who spoke into mine and my sisters' lives. In some cases there were encounters in the mystical realm of both good and evil. There was God intervention too; He released His wisdom, authority, and protection over us through my Aunt Mary and Uncle Charlie (my father's sister) when it came to things of the numinous unseen realm. My mother's brother, Uncle Adolph, had a special gifting in business that just radiated from him with a boldness that is rarely seen in men. Uncle Emanuel and his wife Aunt Mary showed me that love, coupled with wisdom, had "no fear of man." Hattie Fredricks, my great-grandmother on my mother's side, had a way to resolve all conflicts with very little direct words. She could look right through you and at you at the same time, seeing the issue you were dealing with without ever saying anything. With just a few spoken words, everything was settled and peace came into the situation. Her daughter Fannie, my grandmother, was looking after us when we visited, and actually, she was the "normal" grandmother. It was my grandfather Clement Stitt who "saw" many things, and he tried to instruct me. At that time in my mid-teens, I honestly had no clue what he was talking about. It wasn't until later in life as I began to reminisce on that short time we had together that I was able to appreciate what he tried to teach me.

Robinette, my mother's sister, always took me with her to places around the neighborhood. She saw in the mystical realms. We tried to talk a couple of times about it, but there was a big gap between me as a five-year-old child and the young teenage girl. She even broke out the Bible once while attempting to explain to me her spiritual experiences.

This was the last family visit we all had together until we returned from the Orient seven years later.

THE VOICE, *GO PLAY*

There is a God-given movement of steadfastness and grace in Japan. You can feel and see the heavenly presence there.

I sat hiding behind a chair in the late spring of 1967 as I listened to the stories being told by my dad to my mom of unexplainable things that had happened to him and my Uncle Brian while they were in Vietnam. He talked about the favor of God carrying them through many a crisis that could have led to their deaths. He spoke of the friends they left in South Korea. In between the stories, I heard that Uncle Brian received orders to the same base in Japan.

Our families moved to Misawa Air Force Base in the northern part of the island. It was the beginning of the school year for me in grade school. We had Sunday school on Sundays, for those who wanted to attend, and it was held in the school classrooms. The junior high and high school was next door to the base church. Sometimes I would miss the bus intentionally just to walk the three miles to school. I loved the peace that came from these morning walks, and many times would just talk to God, asking Him my many questions.

After living in Japan a few months, I experienced my first natural disaster and a visible angel encounter. He looked like any other person. It was October 1967, and I was sitting at my desk during school working on an assignment. My desk started shaking while I was writing. When I looked up to see what was going on, it had stopped. I went back to writing the assignment when my desk started shaking again. I noticed the boy next to me was shaking the desk. Looking up, I asked the boy to stop shaking the desk and I continued doing my assignment. The desk started shaking again, and this time, without looking up, I snapped at the boy, "Stop!" But now the desk shook more violently, and as I looked over at the boy who was sitting quietly writing at his own desk, I realized the whole building was shaking violently. The teacher shouted, "Get under your desk!" I crawled under the desk as things began to fall from the roof into our classroom. I watched our teacher run out the room, screaming and waving her arms. As I wondered what to do, I began to hear the Voice, *"Go outside and get away from the buildings."*

With that, I stood up, and yelled at the kids in the class, "Go outside, and stay away from the building!"

Then a couple of kids argued back, "But the teacher said to get under our desk!" Suddenly a man appeared at the door of our classroom, and with an urgent voice shouted to the students, "Get outside now...get into your fire rows just like you do for fire drills!" That was the first time I had ever seen this man, and we all watched him go down the hall instructing the next class.

The shaking lasted only about a minute or two, and then it was over. Standing outside now and looking around the grounds of the school, we could see that parts of the roof had collapsed into the building. The ground had cracked wide open across the street, going up the hillsides, with some of those cracks as wide as five feet in a couple of areas. We saw that the corners of some homes had fallen into those wide cracks in the ground. Other homes had collapsed exterior walls. Some of the ground fissures started closing back up fully or at least to some degree, while some parked automobiles and homes had fallen into the fissures.

The students were all accounted for in the fire drill lines. As school resumed a week later, some of the classrooms and corridors were closed because of the "Great Quake" damage. I asked if anyone knew the man who came to the door telling all the children to go outside, but no one knew who he was, and he was never again seen. It makes you wonder if that was an angelic encounter—it will be a question I ask one day when I go to see the Father.

Time moved along in a normal sense, and I was now hitting my preteens.

I enjoyed Sunday school, the choir, and being in the plays. I especially liked the plays where we could hear about and reenact all the Bible stories. We kids talked and dreamed of being like one of those ancient heroes, taking out giants and protecting those in need. We imagined doing the impossible like the conquerors of the past: like Joshua commanding the sun to stand still, Elijah with the elements, Elisha restoring life back into the dead, King David who had a heart of compassion, Peter who had the strength to pursue even after his failure. These stories were etched into our minds as children, preparing us for the adventures ahead. The virtues of God became the values embedded deep inside each of us, and it could be seen by all.

MOTORCYCLES

One sunny spring day, towards the end of sixth grade, some friends asked if I wanted to go motorcycle riding. "Sure, but I don't know how to ride a motorcycle!" I replied.

"Come on," they beckoned, "We'll teach you. It's easy." With this, we all headed off base, going out the side gate into a residential area. We went to a vacant house that looked as if nobody had lived there for years. My friends, Jarvis and Pewee, went around back of the house and brought out a motorcycle they had hidden there. They told me how the two of them had put their money together from doing odd jobs and cutting grass, along with their allowance, and had saved enough to buy this motorcycle without their parents knowing about it. They had learned to ride a motorcycle from the boyfriend of their older sister.

I quickly learned how to ride that motorcycle, but not until I went face first into the dirt a few times. We often rode along wooded trails. I continued to go riding every day after school for weeks with my friends until the motorcycle finally broke down, and no one had money to fix it.

I decided to ask my father if I could have a motorcycle. This question created a whole lot of other questions that my parents wanted answers to.

"How do you know how to ride a motorcycle? When did you learn? Whose bike was it?" After this interrogation by my dad, I persistently asked him for a motorcycle. Then, tired of my insistence, my dad responded, "If you can pay for half of the motorcycle, I will get you one." "Yes, Yes, Yes!" went through my mind as I heard nothing else.

The look on my mother face told a different story, but the word had been given. My mind went to work calculating how to make the money. It was now the second week of June, as school was out for the summer.

Getting up early in the morning, attaching the mower behind my bicycle, I knocked on all the military housing doors inquiring with those residents whose grass was high, "How about if I cut your grass today?"

Some people didn't want their grass cut, but they had other odd jobs for me to do. It was just before the 4th of July weekend that I handed my mother $600 dollars to hold for me, "Do you think this is enough to pay for half of what a motorcycle would cost?"

She was very pleased to see that I earned and saved money. It had never crossed my parents minds that I would earn that much money and so quickly. After purchasing the used motorcycle, my dad took me out to two places on the base where military men rode their off-road motorcycles. One of the riding areas was down by the beach, and the other was on the base next to a war-destroyed military bunker alongside of a decomposed runway that was now only used for marching drills and inspections of troops. The area surrounding the runway was the base forest which had trails and paths that were already being used for motocross riding.

There were also what looked like craters in the ground from bombings. One of the trails led to half circle loops on the sides of the old two-story military bunker. The well-worn trails were clear evidence that this area was being traversed by motorcycles often. The unseen side of the bunker backed up to the woods.

I had been riding at the old airstrip for about a month on some of the trails along the exposed sides of the bunker walls when, on one of those sunny days of motocross riding, we stopped to watch some other riders who had the huge motocross bikes go straight up the corner of the bunker at full throttle and then disappear. I thought to myself, *"I can do that!"* I watched them take off going up that steep grade. I decided to give it a try and readied my bike. "I can do this!" I cried out, talking myself out of the fear I felt in the pit of my stomach.

I revved the motorcycle with the throttle full open and took off zooming up the corner trail to the top. The motorcycle hit the peak of the bunker and flew straight into the air.

The adrenalin was flowing as I looked down for the ground, standing with both feet on the foot pegs, legs bent for the impact of landing. As I was glanced down to see where to land on the roof of the bunker, I saw there was no roof! Instead, the bunker roof laid three stories below in scattered heaps among boulders and rebar protruding out through the overgrown foliage that covered almost everything. Peering down at where I was about to land, fear came over me, and I found I was screaming out for the only thing I knew could help me now, "Oh God, help! Oh God, help...!"

Instantaneously, what seemed to be a pair of gigantic hands appeared and took hold of me with the motorcycle and placed us down on the ground in a small clearing that the trail lead to. It was so far away at such an angle that it would have been impossible for me to land there. I gazed into the sky, having affixed my sight on the hands. I watched the hands vanish the same way they had appeared.

Now in place of the hands and a little higher in the sky, emerged another person—a huge face of a man with long dark hair, a beard, a simple but sincere smile, and a gaze that penetrated deep inside me. As the facial visage changed, the eyes shifted to look another direction in the sky. Turning my gaze to see what the image was looking at, I saw to its right was yet another smaller image. I believe what I was seeing was a guardian angel. The angel resembled a woman in a Victorian-style garment. Breaking its gaze with the huge face, the angel turned to look straight at me as it vanished.

The angel was the last to fade from sight. I gazed at the lingering aura for seconds, minutes, or hours—it was unknown and immeasurable—in awe of what had just transpired. Then as if from a mega speaker from above, I heard the Voice say, "Go play."

I put my helmet back on and got back on the motorcycle to go riding, thanking God all the while as I pondered, "Did I just see God?" To this day I believe I did because if you see Jesus, you have seen the Father.[9]

---

9 John 14:9.

Hoping to see the heavenly images again, I did the run a few more times. I would go up the corner full throttle to the top of the peak. Then come to a rolling stop at the peak as I would coast over inside the corner walls weaving along the trail. I would reach the clearing at the bottom of the trail, stop to get off the motorcycle, and look up at that spot in the sky saying, "Thank you, God!" and remembering that it is not good to test God.

When I got home, I could not wait to tell my friends. The instant I told them about all that had happened, it became a joke among some of my friends. They had no comprehension of my experience. So, I made a point to rarely mention the story to anyone, unless I felt compelled.

INCREASED SPIRITUAL GIFTS

It was during this encounter that I had my first sighting as a seer (Ro'eh). I was twelve years old. This brought along with it the release of other abilities. I knew they were from God and that these abilities were given for a time yet to come. I now had markers for the course. The power coming out of the lighthouse was now brighter in its release, as I was learning to steer.

One such ability manifested itself in a form of what is called "word of knowledge." Similar to 2 Kings 6, I became aware of things before they happened. In the biblical encounter, one of God's prophets, Elisha, warned the king of Israel numerous times with details of attacks the king of Syria planned against Israel. These plans were conceived in the Syrian king's bed chambers; they were secret to all but a few, yet Elisha supernaturally knew them. In this same chapter, you also see how Elisha supernaturally helps a man recover a lost axe head that had sunk to the bottom of a murky river.

After this wonder, sign, and miracle of entrustment from God, there came to me many different types of prophetic and seeing abilities: trances, dreams, translations, and visions. Especially déjà vu, which is a feeling that one has seen or heard something before it happens.

I would know what was about to happen next as though I had lived the event before. There would be times I could whisper under my breath the actions and or words in sync, as I had already seen them take place.

Some friends and I were hanging out one afternoon when a remembrance hit me at the base teen club. Some of them laughed as I told them what was about to happen across the room. I told them that a guy is going to walk in that door and yell at that person over there by the wall. Then the guy who is yelling is going to grab that person by the wall as he tries to move away into that corner by the bar stool. This guy is going to shove him against the pool table, and begin hitting him. All but one of my friends left, going into another part of the club.

Within moments, the scene I described came to life. The guy began raising his fist to hit the other guy who had tried to move. I yelled across the room, "Leave him alone! Pick on someone your own size!" That outburst changed the outcome of the vision. The bully, instead of hitting the guy, turned and came after me and my friend. We just stood there as the bully approached, looked at each other, then turned and ran out the side entrance of the teen club. We were no fools to stick around at thirteen when an older teen was after us.

This is how, without realizing it, I learned of the power of intercession to change outcomes.

By becoming courageous and stepping out, you can actually change an outcome. Interceding is helping, standing in faith, and not just watching. Learn to stand and fight. There are many ways to fight; physical fighting is the most basic.

When I returned to the teen club a little later that day, the bully was still there. He saw me, walked over, and got in my face while my friend moved away. Then another older teen stepped in, telling him to leave us alone. The bully turned, looked at the teen, backed away, and left. This older teen introduced himself as Michael Harris saying, "I was here earlier when you stopped him from hitting that other boy." Michael and I talked, and over the months ahead, we became friends. Michael seemed to be a guardian showing up when I was in over my head interceding for others.

Now and then, my Dad would have what I believed was a word of knowledge, instructing me not to do something or go someplace, but sometimes I would ignore it. My mother use to tell me to just do as Dad says even if it makes no sense. I found over time that he had saved me and others from a lot of trouble and from getting hurt.

Because of the ridicule, over time I refrained from telling people of the word of knowledge insight I experienced unless keeping silent would bring harm to others or I felt compelled to speak. It was over the next couple of years these encounters increased and diminished at the same time. These abilities increased in greater detail on their own accord. When I refrained from using the gift, there was diminishment to a fraction of what I usually receive. When I pursued the revelation, it would at times come back more intense, like turning the hot water faucet up higher for hotter water. I was learning that having the ability to derail situations and to prevent casualties is a very special gift. Virtue is a part of who you are as you step out in any of the gifts of the Holy Spirit.

A new gift emerged as strange images or representations began to appear around a person, people, or things. I saw reflections of hidden emotions, characters of a personality, spiritual bondage, and spiritual attacks, just to name a few. There were times I would hear the Voice or see images which defined what I was seeing, giving me the knowledge needed to handle or speak to the situation.

This new gift of discerning of spirits grew in me as I matured and was able to discern areas of territory, principalities, and rulers. Some people call it an "atmosphere shift," but this is not the same. I saw unclean spirits come into an area, trying to disturb it like gangs trying to control a part of a city area when police are not involved, but the territory would still be under the control of the governing spirit, such as a prince or principality. It was more like a bar room brawl of spirits and demons. With each territorial or governing spiritual disturbance, the losing angelic or demonic spirit was removed and replaced, creating a territorial or regional atmosphere shift. It is like going from a ship to a submarine in the Navy, two totally different territories and atmospheres.

I began to understand that when certain dominating spirits were within my sphere of influence, my mood would shift, picking up its attributes. Sometimes it took a minute to realize the characteristic was not of me. In time, I learned I had the power to rebuke it, sending it on its way or binding it. In Christ Jesus you have the authority and power to deal with these forces.

I was sitting and enjoying a book one day in a coffee shop, when all of sudden some people came in, and I felt the shift. A guy walked by on his way to the restroom, and I felt lustful thoughts jump into my mind. I quickly flicked the thoughts away. There was a group sitting together at a table, and antagonism belonging to one or more of the girls at the table was trying to settle in. This told me that one of them had an anger problem. The thoughts of lust also returned as I listened to one girl talk about going home with the guy. I bound those spirits and told them to go in the name of Jesus, and everything became peaceful again.

In particular regions of countries, I have seen demonic and angelic forces at a faceoff. The principalities were vying for control of the territorial atmosphere as they waited for man's intervention before beginning the fight to take control of that region. I found I could intervene through intercession, prayer, or a simple act before the real engagement would begin; the angelic hosts of heaven did not move or reveal themselves until godly men and or women stepped up to intercede.

What happened during the faceoff was like being a part of a WWF wrestling match. One contender would get thrown out, get up, come back into the ring, and throw the other guy out as this happened a lot with unclean conflicting spirits.

There were times when I was in a region and the Voice told me to leave. I would go into some regional areas seeing more things in the mystical realm than I really wanted to see, along with a strange feeling in my spirit. I would go find a place to rest in the presence of the Lord while praying. A couple of times I was sent to pray simple words, "God, come!" and He came. Many events that took place where not coincidental, but were meant for angelic release that needed a human interaction. The bus ride was an intervention.

BUS RIDE

The seven years I lived in Japan brought many unusual occurrences. The bus ride event happened when my mother and I visited southern Japan. Many military bases where in close proximity to one another, and here is where the medical specialist was located for military personnel and their families. Having arrived at Tachikawa Air Force Base, we settled into the base hotel. Then we were taken by helicopter to another base for an appointment. This ride set a dream in me to learn to fly one day—that is another story for another time.

After returning, I took a bus ride to one of the joining bases to see a movie. Throughout the ride, a group of older teens was harassing me. They stayed in my face, but I ignored them. Finally, they got off the bus. The very next stop, just before I got off the bus, a group of guys introduced themselves as brothers and friends. Their leader said to me, "We had your back in case those guys started a fight with you."

It was almost a year later that I was back in southern Japan for an in-and-out surgery. I caught the bus again going to the movie theater, but this time I started harassing some people on the bus about something that happened. The people just ignored me until eventually they got off the bus. Once they departed, a young man stood up in the back of the bus. Surrounded by his friends, he looked me in the eyes and said, "You were wrong...if anything had happened, we would have stood up for them...you were wrong."

I then realized it was the same person with his brothers and friends who stood up for me about a year ago. I followed them off the bus, walking and talking with them all the way to their house where we said our goodbyes. The next day I retraced my steps from the bus stop going back to the young man and his brother's house. I felt such a connection between the young man and I as he talked; I wanted to know him better. It was like when the two disciples were walking on the road to Emmaus:

Did not our hearts burn within us while he talked to us on the road? (Luke 24:32)

An older man answered my knock on the door. When I asked the man if his sons were at home, he informed me that he had no sons and no boys lived there. I asked more questions but the man only replied, "No such people live around the neighborhood." I'm sure it was this house that I walked them to the night before; I showed the man the piece of paper I had written the house number on. Again, he replied, "Sorry..." as he shut the door. I walked around asking the neighbors about these guys, but no one knew any such young men.

Cogitating on the way back to the bus stop, I checked and rechecked all the reference points along the path to the house. This was a second meeting almost a year apart on a bus with the same people who waited in the background for a potential outcome to be decided and in whose favor to proceed; this was neither a norm nor a coincidence. My question to this day is, *were these boys angels walking among us in disguise?*

This encounter also reminded me of Joshua and the commander of the Lord's army:

A man was standing before him with his drawn sword in his hand. And Joshua went to him and said to him, "Are you for us, or for our adversaries?" **14** *And he said, "No; but I am the commander of the army of the Lord. (Joshua 5:13-14)*

This incident set precedence in me to stand up for those in need. This would at times lead to physical fights in protecting people. I always made sure the person I defended was in the right and tried to first look for a peaceful solution, but at times, there was none to be found. I never threw the first blow, but retaliated as I saw it coming just before impact.

I thought wrestling would be a good skill for defending. So, in my freshman year of high school, I tried out for the wrestling team and made the junior varsity team at 129 pounds. Later that season, the door opened for me to take a varsity position at 129 pounds. I grew in strength and agility. My Dad was always telling me, "Stop sticking up for people! Let them fight their own battles," but I knew what I had to do.

My dad told me to observe other people before making any decision on what to do. He said,

"You will not listen to me, so see for yourself how people's lives turn out from what they do."

Learning by observing the outcome of other people's choices or mistakes became a habit.

There were a lot of youth I knew doing drugs or drinking, being forced by peer pressure to try to fit in. Dad's advice kept me from doing drugs; I observed that those who did drugs were in real need of help. If they didn't actually kill you, these addictions could cripple you and others for life in many ways. The phrase "*steal, kill and destroy*"[10] has great meaning as it relates to addiction.

My family's seven years of service in Japan had finished, and it was time to relocate to Michigan for my sophomore year and my dad's last year in the military.

These stories are reference points for understanding in how to walk in spiritual giftings. The occult will call on you, and you have the power to send it on its way through Christ. The Holy Spirit and angelic hosts of Heaven will intercede through you and for you if you ask.

---

10 John 10:10 The thief comes only to steal and kill and destroy

Chapter Four

THE DEVELOPMENT

OUR SEVEN-YEAR MILITARY tour in Japan was over, and my Dad received what would be his final orders before his retirement to go to Kincheloe Air Force Base. Prior to that, we decided to take a vacation and visit our relatives since we had not seen them since arriving in Japan.

It was amazing how my cousin Robinette and I reconnected after all those years. By this time, she was twenty and I was fifteen, and yet, even with the age difference, there was a strong spirit of understanding between us that went beyond normal maturity. She was a young woman now and had the experience that comes from growing up in a big city. She would often say to me, "Soon enough, you will understand me."

We were inseparable during this family visit and spent time together right up until she had to go to work each day. I began to recognize that I was seeing the same things in the Spirit that she was seeing as we traveled here and there together in Chicago. We would often compare what we were seeing in the unseen dimensions as we crossed the city on the overhead "L" trains. The mystical and natural phenomena throughout the city reflected each other. In some regions of the city, it was like we were watching supernatural movies in action in the mystical realms. Robinette told me she had confided in our Grandma Hattie, sharing her ability to see in the supernatural realm, and would often tell her what she was seeing. Since Grandma Hattie had passed away, my cousin had not shared this with other family members for fear of ridicule.

But now as we were together, we began to appreciate the ability that others did not have to "see" things. We could see spiritual battles over territories taking place in every region of the city, and though Robinette and I experienced it in different ways, the interpretation was always the same. As a youth, seeing in this way was kind of cool yet frightening at the same time. I had no one to give understanding to what I was seeing, and I had no frame of reference except my own experiences, but now I could share these things with my cousin. It was a bit of an adjustment for me coming out of pond-simple experiential knowledge into a great lake of unnatural mystification and learning to adapt to this greater place. I felt like a fish out of water.

I had an experience at this time that really stood out to me. One day, I was alone coming back to my uncle's home while taking the "L" train, and I accidently missed the stop. I took the next exit about a mile further down knowing I would have to walk back to the house. As I descended the platform steps to the street, I suddenly felt as if blinders were removed from my eyes. The things I saw happening in the mystic realm in that moment sent shivers through me like never before. I saw what was getting ready to happen as well as what was already happening in both the spiritual and physical realms. Everything seemed to be heightened within me.

Then all of a sudden, what must have been a spirit realized that I was able to see it, and so it turned and started walking towards me from across a four-lane street directly under the rail system. This frightened me so much that I took off running the full mile all the way back to my Uncle Emanuel's house.

As I was running down the sidewalk, I could see different characteristics that some of the spirits represented. I saw good and evil, joy, hate, abuse, etc. In each block, the spirits were of different sizes and shapes on both sides of the street. The spirit which was moving my direction stopped after three blocks as if it was not allowed to cross any further. It watched while I kept it in view, looking over my shoulder from the sidewalk as it just stood there in the middle of the street. There were also what appeared to be warriors dressed in plain clothes and standing in designated positions, but not revealing themselves. I passed by them knowing somehow nothing could prevail against them. They were standing there with an authority—looking at me and right through me—with a kind of smile as I passed by them.

Later on, I considered what had just happened and thought to myself, "If this is what Robinette has to deal with in Chicago, it can't be easy." I began to realize that many seers, especially those living in larger cities or certain areas of high mystical activity, seem to have a serious drug and/or alcohol abuse problem or they are often recruited by these evil spirits that I saw to participate in the occult realm.

Prophetic people have a genuine need to communicate with others who have similar abilities. In time, many have focused using their gifts in a business career and have actually become quite successful. I began to realize that when you receive a revelation, reaching deeper is required because of what is needed for the final outcome.

There are unclean spirits that hide behind their relative spirits when someone with authority and power shows up. This is especially true with such spirits as prejudice, deception, and hate. The opposite of these are the spirits of understanding, truth, love, peace, and joy, and when those are released into the spiritual atmosphere, the Lord's angelic hosts are then sent as reinforcements to uphold His authority in these realms. At such times there are ministering angels sent, others are messengers, and some are sent as warrior angels.

MINDSETS

We need greater understanding and revelation of the Scripture, *"We do not fight against flesh and blood but against principalities, authorities, and rulers."*[11] The renewing of our mind about what is

---

11 Ephesians 6:12.

continually going on in the realm all around us has the ability to transform who we really are and enable us to mature in that role.

Many of our great-grandparents were taught from birth the mindset of slavery and poverty while living alongside the stark contrast of the "superiority" of wealth. This contrast was clearly evident in most cities across America and continued to create a strong polarization of people groups even since the time of the Civil War. During that time in US history, the spirit of slavery was actually an evil principality, ruler, and authority until it (and other like-spirits) was dethroned by God through the people who had been wronged. Through such people as Dr. Martin Luther King, Jr., and others who saw slavery as the evil that it was, the enslaved were able to grab hold of the "dream" that would set them free from bondage. God will always find those who will see in a nation the evil ruling principalities which have created oppressive poverty conditions and who are willing to partner with Him and pay the price to overthrow their authority and see transformation. That is one of the values of the seer gift.

The gifting allows those willing to partner with Jesus to bring healings in physical health issues as well as issues that cannot be seen, such as mental traumas or a broken spirit, thus bringing back life in the person or community. Trauma can open a door for evil spirits to kill, steal, or destroy, as those spirits sink their grips into the person or community. Sometimes this demonic involvement manifests as a physical injury. The only thing I have found that frees and heals a person or people is an intentional act of forgiveness and mercy. This grace, which is a gift that comes from God, has the ability to release those who are willing to forgive and extend mercy. It is that simple. Forgiveness enables a person to live life to the fullest through love, and God provides His grace freely to those who desire it.

The slavery imposed on America by evil men had created prejudices in many different forms, and with it came many other evil "relatives" with other principalities. For decades since the abolition of slavery, we have taught our children that slavery of any kind is wrong, along with all of its ugly forms of prejudices; as we teach this truth, we are literally destroying that principality and ruler along with its relatives. We cannot down play it by reducing it to less than what it really is by calling it something like chauvinism or narrow-mindedness. Doing this could actually cause prejudice to grow once again. The key here is to let love continue to transform the way we think and never allow prejudice of any kind to rear its ugly head and become a stronghold in our minds or in our nation. Finding ways to continually renew our minds and develop a greater love for one another is the better way.

The Apostle Paul says:

Do not be fashioned according to this world: but be ye transformed by the renewing of your mind, and ye may prove what is the good and acceptable and perfect will of God. (Romans 12:2)

Even if you do not believe in God, transforming your mind is essential to living better. Without this transforming of our minds, we cannot mature fully as people, and we cannot mature spiritually if we harden our hearts.[12] This is a law with scientists as they reach towards major breakthroughs in the advancements of science. If I had closed my mind and not forgiven those of prejudiced nature, many destructive things could have happened, as you will see in subsequent chapters of this book.

At this new Air Force base in Northern Michigan, out in the middle of nowhere, there were people of Indian decent, blacks, and many other minority races, all having to overcome many obstacles. In a sense, it was similar to the cast system of India. Here in this often hostile environment, evil principalities reared up and revealed their ugliness.

---

12 Ephesians 4:18, Hebrew 4:16

RUDYARD

The high school I would attend was in Rudyard, a very small town 10 miles from the base. Winter was approaching fast. Since it wasn't possible to ride a motorcycle in the winter with six feet snow on the ground, I asked my dad about purchasing a snowmobile. "Well, I'll think about it," was his response.

A few weeks passed, and one day my father surprised us all when he came home early from work.

"Ray, I have a surprise for you," my dad called out. He had bought me a Yamaha 400cc snowmobile! I was so surprised. "You can use it when I don't need it for work."

It was during these years that I was actually dreaming of the idea of becoming a brain surgeon or a scientist one day. My personality had developed in such a way that I was rather extreme at whatever it was that I was pursuing. One of my favorite things to do at this time was to go to the base gym, and it was there that I began taking lessons in martial arts. This was definitely a defining moment for me personally as this art form became very much a part of my life.

Walking down the school hallway one day, my eye caught a light shining down on a freshman girl. She had beautiful, fair skin which reminded me of Ivory, and shoulder-length brunette hair that she kept flipping out of her face. I was so curious about the light that I went up to her.

"Hi. I'm Ray. What's your name?"

She introduced herself to me and seemed glad that I talked to her. "Hi, I'm Denise. I live up the street from you!" she told me, flipping her hair out of her face, she was pretty. Boy, did I feel dumb. We began to hang out together after that and actually become good friends. In time, I confided in her about the things I saw in the spirit realm. I was always looking for other people who might give me clues as to why I was seeing the things that I did. I was fast realizing that this was indeed an unusual gift, not common among my family and peers.

I really got everyone's attention one day while we were in the Candy Shack, a little shack on the front lawn of our high school. There the student body sold candy, treats, and other food items during lunch break. Suddenly, I experienced one of those *déjà vu* moments. I told Denise what was about to happen any moment just outside.

I turned around and announced to everyone, "Stay inside the store! Some red neck guys are about to drive by and cause some trouble here. They will be pointing their rifles out of their vehicle, yelling and cursing ethnic vulgarities at anyone who is not white! Stay inside the shack!"

Oh the look on the face of one couple who turned to walk out, but then, within a second of stepping out of the store, dived back into the shack! Sure enough, it happened just as I had foreseen. We all watched in shock as the vehicle drove in front of the high school. Peering out from behind the cracked door and through the window of the shack, we could all see these guys had two rifles pointed out their car windows. We could see other weapons pointed out as well. The men in the car were randomly shooting and calling out curses to the students. Thankfully, no one was injured by the stray bullets. Later, we heard that those involved in this hateful attack had been caught and reprimanded.

Immediately after this incident, I began to recall memories of when I was about four to five years old in the sandbox watching my mother's tears fall as she comforted me after the hate-filled words spoken to me by our neighbor. I remembered what she said to me then, and I realized that it was an appropriate response in this situation as well: "*That lady was sick and needed help!*" Wise words indeed. People with prejudice and hate are sick, and they need help.

THE SHIFT

From that day forward, I determined within myself, "*I will stand up and show people that prejudice is a sickness, we are all create equal and there is a cure!*" They will learn there is a cure.

It was at that point in my life I realized that spirits of bondage prevalent on people could not hide from my sight. I watched as spirits tried to sink their claws into people, but I also observed the power of love with its supernatural ability to stop these claws from being embedded deeper into the person. No matter how hard people tried to hide the sickness of prejudice and hate, I could always see it.

It was also from this time on that other images emerged that I was able to identify with clarity. One day, as I sat looking out the school hallway window at the football stadium bleachers, I saw a girl just sitting there. I walked out the side door and headed toward her. I noticed then that she had a razor in her hand. I knew she was contemplating cutting her wrists. I sat down with her there on the stadium bleachers just to engage a conversation, and we talked for some time. When it was time for me to leave, I told her how special and very gifted she was. I was feeling these things for her from a deep place inside of me and knew I had to tell her.

"You know, if you cut your wrists, you will miss out on all the things you were planning to do. You will miss meeting all the people who are supposed to be in your life. So many people will miss out on your being here…"

With those simple words of truth spoken into her life, I turned to leave. Then, hearing her speak to me, I turned my head to look at her directly. "You are a blessing…thank you," she said.

I smiled back to her in response, then headed back into the school. Once inside, I stopped to look out the window to see that she had gotten up to leave. Later that day, I found out this young girl was actually the girlfriend of one of the young men in the vehicles with the weapons. She introduced him to me when I saw her after school one time.

The winds of change where blowing.

After school one day, I was at home flipping through TV channels and came upon a documentary about the Himalayan

Mountains and Tibet which captured my immediate attention. While watching the documentary, I heard the Voice say, "That will be your training ground." This word sent a pulse through my whole body which made me quiver.

At the time, I was thinking that the Lord might be talking about karate as I had come to really love the sport. This prophetic word of the Lord would be on my heart for decades to come as I continued training in martial arts, always looking for an open door into Tibet and the Himalayas—which did begin to unfold three decades later. I also recalled what my dad use to tell me and my sisters.

You can do anything if you put your mind to it. Don't let anyone tell you that you can't.

Learn everything that you can from a teacher whether you like them as a person or not. Learn what they know.

You will never know unless you try.

Be a leader, not a follower.

These words became a marker for direction as they echoed through my heart and mind.

Time went on, and I changed direction. I began to think about doing the "cool" things my teenage peers were doing. I wanted to be an adult.

With the fake ID I managed to secure and the snowmobile, going to buy beer and Boones Farm wine by the case had become a routine for me. One cold winter weekend night, Denise and I, along with a group of other friends, were sitting on wooden crates around a blazing bonfire. The ground was already covered with a few feet of snow, but we kept warm by the crackling fire just talking about the future and sharing our dreams with one another.

Denise, looking down at my quivering hands asked, "Ray, are you cold?

"No," I said. Passing the bottle of Boones Farm wine around, someone called out, "Hey Ray, what do you want to be when you get older?"

Without hesitation I responded, "Brain surgeon." With that, I was instantly drawn into a trance where I heard the Voice say, "You have to have steady hands if you want to do brain surgery. You have to have skilled hands."

Then just as suddenly, I was back again from the trance and looking down at my hands which were shaking. In that moment, I realized that there was no way I could perform surgery with hands that shook as violently as mine. I tried to steady my hands, but to no avail. The beer and wine continued to flow. Friends around me were laughing and joking. The fire burned hot, warming us all. But I was away…reflecting on the truth of the words that had just been seared into my spirit. *You have to have skilled hands.*

I looked down at my shaking hands. I knew why they were shaking…it was from all the drinking I had been doing on the weekends with my friends.

"Hey Ray! Don't you have to have steady hands to be a brain surgeon?" With that everyone roared with laughter. The absurdity of what I knew I was meant to be and what I was living hit me hard, but my pride had been stung.

I yelled over the laughter of my friends, "I have steady hands!" and with that, jerked off my gloves to reveal my future surgeon's hands before them all. Through the fire's reflection I could see their bleary eyes watching me intently as I tried to steady my trembling hands but could not. Now they mocked me all the more with their laughter. Standing before them as I looked around the circle, the words of my Dad's wisdom came flooding to mind. I knew I was observing the traits of those who were alcoholics, drug addicts, and even ex-alcoholics—the shakes that often occur in a body after years of abuse.

The sting hit me full force. In that moment, I put my head down and prayed, "God, I promise I will stop all my drinking if I can please just have my steady hands back." Pausing to think this prayer through since I did not ever want to break a promise to God, I added, "Except for just once in a while on special occasions. Amen."

I knew my prayer was heard and God had released the answer because at that very instant, my hands became straight and stopped shaking. They were so strong and firm that I reached over and grabbed some logs to throw on the fire.

I looked straight up at everyone in that circle and said, "I will be a brain surgeon with skilled hands." Denise smiled at me in agreement as she grabbed on to my arm and held it tight.

This event ended and so did all of my wine and beer buying as well as drinking with my friends. I threw away my fake ID. From then on, I was true to my promise to God, and Dad's advice was foremost in my mind and heart:

Be better than me. Do better than I have. That will make me happy and you a better person.

Always learn what someone knows or is willing to teach you because one day you may need it or someone else may need it as you become the teacher.

Always be strong minded, not weak minded. Think for yourself. Be the leader not a follower.

I went back to bringing down barriers of racism through acts of love and grace as God gave me opportunity. The year passed, and it was time to leave Michigan. My Dad would be retiring to Northern California, and the move would be bringing new adventures to be explored.

DNA GIFTINGS

This capability of seeing in dimensions of time and space through visions, dreams, and translations works together with a person's natural abilities. Natural and supernatural gifts coincide with evolution in our God-designed DNA. In the natural, we have to be adjusted either by man-made physical enhancements, evolution, or by the Holy Spirit. We learn to care for one another more as we understand that everyone has different abilities and gifts. It is the Lord's Spirit that distributes the release. The Spirit checks our hearts continuously so we do not harm ourselves or others. The desires of your heart can also activate supernatural abilities. We are learning to understand and receive words of knowledge in many forms.

This statement is good in teaching us about transforming our thoughts for growth.

If you receive a prophet as a prophet you receive a prophet's reward and if you receive a righteous man as a righteous man you receive a righteous man's reward. (Matthew 10:41)

One thing the passage is saying is that you can learn from someone else's experience of taking the easy road or you can take the hard road by ignoring words of wisdom and counsel. We always have a choice, and it is our personal choices that define who we are. The Holy Spirit will give us the opportunity to correct a mistake if we realize we made one. This said, it is always good to ask for help from Holy Spirit in correcting the mistake. Remember, each day we can start afresh and anew.

Just as in my experience at the bonfire, I was healed of my shaking hands because I asked. How could Jesus tell us to forgive our brothers and sisters seventy times seven if He himself did not see that is what our Father was doing:

He [Jesus] only does what He sees the Father doing. (John 5:19-20)

I would recommend that you take the time to write down the times you ask for help. Then ask the Lord to show you His hand at work in that situation where you needed help. Consider what happened after you asked. I would like to pray for you now.

Father God, I ask you to show the reader and others who ask for help that You reveal to them Your hand at work in their situation. I ask You to place in their heart a desire to be one who is willing to step out in grace and love for one another, knowing we all need grace. Let their hearts and their families hearts be revitalized with a new and fresh touch of Your Spirit. Let Your peace and joy rest in them and around them. One more thing I ask, Father, is that You will increase the abilities in those whose hearts have a desire to see. Give them the stength to walk the path You designed for them. In Jesus name, Amen.

Chapter Five
CONSEQUENCES WITH FAVOR

BY THE TIME I WAS a junior in high school, I was a new student attending Fairfield High School in Northern California, and I began asking people to recommend a good karate school for me. Karate to me was a sport with such graceful movements, similar to ballet, as it cannot be defined in definitive moves, per se, but rather, had to be felt with each technique. In karate, you and the flowing movement of techniques become one. This was how I imagined the mighty men of King David to function. Eleazar[13], Jashobeam[14], and Gadites[15], and even the least of them could each take on a hundred enemies single-handedly as the Spirit ushered through them.

Another year passed in our new location and different adventures created new learning experiences that were preparing me for my future. My senior year began by taking many surprising turns. By keeping my heart right, I saw alternatives to what was developing to make the outcome better than what was common.

One such reflection is the time I was caught in the middle of racial riots. Guamanians and Whites went up against Blacks, Koreans, and Filipinos. I was right in the middle of it, having been pulled in by the police and elected as one of the leaders to help put an end to the conflict. That situation, in time, actually created friendships between the nationalities and two rival high schools in town.

---

13 2Samuel 23:9
14 1Chronicles 11:11
15 1Chronicles 12:14

As for you, you meant evil against me, but God meant it for good, to bring it about that many people* should be kept alive, as they are today. (Genesis 50:20)

Having graduated and moved out at seventeen, things got even deeper in the natural and in the supernatural.

HOT SUMMER NIGHTS

In the late 1970s, on a hot, summer night, I was hanging out with friends and cruising up and down the main strip in one of their muscle cars, a 1969 SS Camero. At one point, we pulled over, got out of the car, and were just engaged in conversation while watching the other muscle cars traveling along the strip. I heard the Holy Spirit say very clearly to me: "Do not get back into that car. You are to stay right where you are."

The other two guys I was with decided to get back into the car to go cruising again, but having been warned by the Holy Spirit, I tried to persuade the others to stay with me. They choose not to listen to me and drove off. I went on home, but in the early morning hours, a police officer came to the trailer where I lived and told me about an automobile accident my two friends had been in. This officer had heard from others that I had been with these friends earlier that evening. He told me that the owner of the car was dead and the other one was in the hospital in critical condition. In time, my friend recovered completely from the physical trauma he incurred, but this experience actually crippled the survivor for life in many other ways.

People often experience doubts when they hear a word of warning, but the pain and cruelty that can come from the decisions we make, even in light of those warnings, is something I couldn't comprehend. There are many who disbelieve the obvious truth of a word even when it is right in front of them, and some choices made in that unbelief are serious enough to sustain irreversible damage. Over the years, I have learned that it is not for the prophetic person to hold himself responsible after he delivers the message. The one who receives a message of warning from the Holy Spirit is obliged to give it, but he is not responsible for the outcome if those who hear it intentionally ignore it. As it states in Matthew 10:

> *And if anyone will not receive you or listen to your words, shake off the dust from your feet when you leave that house or town.*

The more a seer sees and delivers messages, the more effective he or she becomes in communicating, but in the end, it is always left to the receiver's choice. This seer ability might actually be more effective with one-on-one and smaller groups. It is our decisions that define situations and us individually or as a group. The numinous events become a normal affair in the prophetic.

NIGHT OF DANCING

Going back to high school times, as a teen, I loved to go dancing. One weekend, I was going dancing with some friends in Vallejo, a town about 18 miles away from where I lived. Henry, whose family is from the Philippines and a great martial artist, along with some of the other guys, was getting ready to go outside. Then, instantly, I went into a trance seeing guys with guns outside in cars shooting at them. I grabbed Henry and pulling him to the side, I said to him, "Stay inside the dance right now. No need to go outside. Let's go check out those girls."

Suddenly we heard gun shots coming from outside, and the other guys came running back inside the dance hall from the lobby where they had been waiting for Henry. From inside the hall we heard cars squealing off down the street. When we reached the outside of the building to see what was happening, people were ducked down behind objects and, amazingly, no one was hurt even though bullets had riddled the building.

This prophetic experience was similar yet a bit different than past times. I figured if I kept talking to Henry about girls instead of trying to persuade him to stay in the dance hall, that it might work, and it did. There is no set pattern to what I receive prophetically and how I deliver it. It is like trial and error, and you learn to use what is in front of you at that moment. There are no books or people to rely on in the moment, only the Holy Spirit, my friend.

By this time in high school, I had begun to play football. One day, before going to practice, I see this freshman girl with blond hair and blue eyes in a white T-shirt and blue overalls standing by the locker room of the gym. A beam of light streamed down from the heavens and engulfed her. I blurted out boldly to my friend, "That is what I am talking about as being fine…that's fine. She is fine!"

"Later bro!" I called out to my friend Foots and walked over to introduce myself to the girl.

"Hello, I'm Lorrie," she said to me. As I looked at her I heard, "As a flower blooming sweet with purity." Whether the sound was in the natural or spiritual, I don't know. She had a personality that was sweeter than honey. We talked, and the more we talked, the more heavenly things became around her. I had never seen anyone sweeter or more pure than her. Over the next few days, we started becoming close at school.

I walked Lorrie home from school and met up with her stepfather, Ron, one day at the door of their home. In the spiritual realm, I saw mystical creatures hovering over her stepfather, ruler types that take control of a person's life and destroy everything. These types of spirits clings to different types of leaders with issues that have caused them to harden their hearts, but the victims are ignorant that these spirits have dug their claws deep into them. I watched them as I reached out to shake hands with him, "Hello!"

I looked him in the eye, and he intentionally ignored me, leaving my hand just hanging in the air. He was sending a clear signal that he wanted nothing to do with me. So, I told him goodbye, and left the house. I felt such bigotry and hate coming from him which clearly was because of his past and had probably caused his alcohol dependency. I have seen those same spirits attach themselves to people, destroying the health of some and the lives of others.

The only way to get rid of the things that have attached themselves is through God's love transforming our lives and our minds. We need to forgive and ask for forgiveness from God in Jesus' name. This breaks any opened access for unclean spirits and sets a person free. With freedom comes healing, peace, joy, and a new life.

The following day, Lorrie told me that she had an argument with her stepfather about our relationship and that she was not allowed see me anymore because of my ethnicity. Shortly after that, her family moved to Sacramento.

We each make our own choices, but God has a plan for each of us as you will see.

HEALING WITHIN

Shortly after this, I started going to parties again, not to do drink or do drugs, but I suppose because I was young and just wanted to have fun. I chose to hang out with the radicals and rebels. I didn't consider these people as the wrong crowd. To me, these were the ones who liked to have fun and had little or no fear in trying new things. I viewed them as guys and gals who would not be spayed or neutered by society. Throughout history, these were the type of men and women who arose up when the time for societal change emerged; until such a time, however, they were regarded as outcasts. Some of these so-called rebels actually became great leaders after the youth of their day initiated a new way of thinking.

Consider these "radical" men of their day who went on to bring significant contributions to their generation: Teddy Roosevelt, General (Mad Dog) Smith, General Patton, William Penn, Samuel Adams, Amelia Earhart, Albert Einstein, Martin Luther King Jr., the Wright Brothers, and Steve Jobs, to name a few. What we do with the time we have can improve society and change lives.

During those years I came to know one such rebel, a young man by the name of William (Bill) Kienzle. He was a knight to many. Bill was a character combination of Fonzie from the '70's TV show "Happy Days," and the movie character Raggedy Man (Mad Max) in the movie "Road Warrior Episodes" in which actor Mel Gibson played.

I learned from Bill that friendship goes beyond just words; it's in the "doing." Like the Scripture says,

Be doers of the word, not hearers only, deceiving yourselves. (James 1:22)

Bill's friendship really taught me this. There was a time, I recall, when I was riding through town with Bill in his 1969 SS Camero, when suddenly, he swung his car over to the side of the road, jumped out the car, and rushed to the side of a homeless man who was being shoved around by some teens. He got right in their faces and sent them on their way. Returning to his car and grabbing his money, he gave it to the homeless man. Bill was always an example of character for everyone. Bill demonstrated in his everyday life what it meant to live as a godly man.

Over time, our "group" became known as "4 Barrels," a type of modern day knights of the late '70s and '80s. We got the name from building hot rods and drag racing. When we punched down on the pedal, the carburetors could be heard kicking in to win the races. The "4 Barrels" were known as the ones to protect and watch over those in trouble, especially many at parties.

It was during these times I would hear the Voice more often instructing me with such promptings as, "Go into the house." I would obey and walk through the house, for example, and inevitably find a guy or girl trying to take advantage of someone who was not in their right mind due to substance abuse. We would then intercede to protect them.

One of the hardest times for me was when a girl confided in me that her father was molesting her. She happened to be the daughter of a high-ranking public official, and I had no idea where to go or what to do about it. I tried to help, but to no avail. I went to counselors about her situation without revealing identity, but they all told me to go to the authorities. In this case, her parent was in charge of the authorities. Because I was only a teenager and I was helpless. Not knowing what to do, I simply started avoiding her. The fact that I was not able to make a difference in her life haunted me for years.

This incident changed me, and I began looking for individuals of strength and wisdom to associate with. I began to see the importance of knowledge. The list of what I wanted in a companion and or wife that my 2nd grade teacher talked about[16] began to echo through my mind as I started adding to its values from my own personal experiences.

- No liars or lying, period
- No drunks/alcoholics
- No drug users
- Truthful
- Loyalty
- Faithful/no cheaters
- Honesty
- Loving
- No smokers
- ?

---
16 Chapter 3 page 34

The hard choice to do or not do something often comes at a crossroads, and it seems that it is never at a convenient time. We often have a choice: to help or go have fun. My conscience would always turn me around, even if I chose fun over someone I didn't like to help. Two more years of hearing the Voice and seeing into the spirit realm went by, and I was beginning to realize more and more how much I needed a better life—to stop living the way I was. At the time, I was working for a seasonal company and didn't realize that I should put money away for the season of slow business. Very soon, I wound up living on the street, but only for a short time. I asked my parents if I could move back home for a while, and shortly thereafter, I joined the Marine Corp. I was glad to be a part of a company of people known as "the few, the proud, the elite."

As I left for the Marine Corp Recruit Depot in San Diego, my dad gave me this advice: "Do not volunteer for anything, and Do not be a Hero." Then I heard the Voice say, "*Observe everything.*" It was from the complex to the simple working standards of the Corp I watched and learned. I found that I really excelled in the civilian work force training program, and I advanced to be the platoon leader during that time. My platoon achieved great recommendations from the civilians in charge of the work programs. During war games, I volunteered to aid the senior drill instructor. He taught his volunteers "out of the box" thinking, and we won the war games in record-breaking time. My dad often use to tell me,

Be open-minded and adaptable to all situations. Do not close your mind; be open-minded.

I learned that the choices we make determine how we grow and connect. There is always a reason the Holy Spirit releases the abilities. They sometimes create unsolved mysteries, but always leave a sign pointing to Jesus.

Having graduated basic training, I went on into the Marine Corp Electrical Engineering School as an electrician, receiving orders to the 8th Communication Battalion Camp in Lejuene, North Carolina. After being at my post for a year, I received acclaim from my superiors for outstanding work as an electrician, and they sent me back to Advance Electrical Engineering School to become a journeyman electrician. This educational offer usually comes to those with 4 to 5 years' experience as an electrician.

In those first couple of years at Lejuene, I worked with another marine, a surfer from Virginia named Burrows. He was a godly man, honorable and a hard-working. Burrows truly loved surfing, and I would see him always reading the Bible when he wasn't studying or surfing. One evening, with his surfboard and Bible in hand, he headed to the beach at the end of one of those long, summer days. Stopping him in the hall, I asked, "Burrows, why do you always carry your Bible surfing?"

Looking me in the eye, he responded, "I seem to comprehend God's word better after surfing," and he turned to continue out to the beach. His comment stirred something inside of me, and because of it, I decided to read the Bible in its entirety from beginning to end.

As I worked through reading the Bible, I eventually came to Matthew 22 and really took to heart something that Jesus said.

> *Teacher, which is the great commandment in the Law? And he said to him, "You shall love the Lord your God with all your heart and with all your soul and with all your mind. This is the great and first commandment. And a second is like it: You shall love your neighbor as yourself. On these two commandments depend all the Law and the Prophets."* (Matthew 22:36-40)

This directive gave me something simple to follow without any "wind of doctrine." If I knew nothing else, I knew these verses were the keys for me personally.

THE R&R

A military-granted time off is fondly referred to as "R&R." My seer realm had been on an R&R for a while, but it seemed to be emerging again. I was experiencing a release of words of knowledge for physical healings along with a few other revelations.

When on military R&R, I would often take off in my car and head north or south along the coast, depending on the time of year. One weekend I decided to go to Boston to visit my Aunt Mary and Uncle Charlie. When I arrived, I found my cousin Danny was living back in Boston. Danny was on his way to a dance club out in the Cape of Massachusetts, and he asked if I wanted to join him. Always looking for some fun, I agreed, and the two of us were enjoying our time together. Suddenly, the atmosphere changed in the dance club, but I seemed to be the only one who noticed. I felt unclean spirits were looking to invade or engage here, and I knew that it would soon manifest in the natural. Immediately, my inner defenses went to a heightened alert. I felt it was time to go; I was not able to see the unclean spirits, but could feel their presence and knew this was unfamiliar territory to me. I knew enough from my past experience to know that what I was feeling was a warning. I prayed for heavenly intervention. This was the presence of an entity I had never felt before.

I found my cousin and urged him to leave, but he would not. So, I left Danny at the club and spent the night with another cousin on the Cape. The next day I picked Danny up at the club and learned that there had been knife fights shortly after I left. Thankfully, no one was killed. Along the entire drive back to Boston, Danny told me the story of what happened after I left him at the club.

Many months later, I went back for another visit to Cape Code. This time Danny and I went out on a party ship that was doing a Cape Verdean event. I experienced the exact same presence out in the middle of the bay, but being on a ship, I could not leave. Instead, I interceded to stop the manifestations in the natural. I released commands into the atmosphere in the party hall and on the deck of the ship. Within twenty minutes everyone was back to enjoying themselves. I saw that there were a few people who were very angry because the spirits had been bound and they had been immobilized—not able to speak or move—and could only just sit there. I pondered the last time I had felt this unclean presence and wondered to myself, *should I have stayed at the club and changed things the last time?*

During one R&R weekend, I went south on to Savannah, Georgia, the home of my Aunt Ruby and Uncle Bryan who was now retired from the Air Force. My uncle had an understanding of putting everything into its proper place, and I sought his wisdom about dealing with military issues. Aunt Ruby would not say much, a woman of few words, but when she did speak, it was with great counsel and valuable wisdom. Whoever listened would be enlightened on how to achieve or correct any given situation.

This knowledge I received from my family could not be taught, this wisdom only comes through experience. It was godly wisdom, as if it came direct from the Lord himself. I grasped ahold of these wise words like dry sponge absorbing water.

The next week, having returned to work, I was once again dealing with prejudice and the narrow-mindedness of the gunnery sergeant in charge of my engineering unit. The R&R weekend full of godly wisdom from my family had come at a perfect time, and I was making full use of it in this situation.

HOLDING YOU TO YOUR WORD

On one of those hot, humid days so common in North Carolina, a crate was delivered to the electrical shop. I began opening this crate which was about 4½ feet tall and wide. It had been heavily nailed shut and was difficult to open. I went to the tool room to retrieve an S-shaped crowbar to open the crate. Taking off my camouflage shirt, I worked on the crate in my white undershirt.

Finally the top of the crate popped off, and I then began working on one of the sides of the crate. I hammered one of the claws of the crow bar into the joint between the sides while pulling on the crow bar. I was getting frustrated, though, because it just would not open. Putting a foot against the bottom of the crate while simultaneously pulling on the crow bar, the corner joint abruptly gave way and the other end of the claw came slamming into the side of my head, implanting itself right between my temple and left ear. Falling against the crate from the impact, I was dizzy from the blow. I pulled on the end of the crow bar but realized that it was implanted in the side of my head. Leaning against the crate and trying to regain composure, I was trying to figure out what to do. Blood was running down the side of my face from the deep laceration. Here I was, bleeding from my head and trying to contemplate whether to go to the medical clinic or not. I really dislike hospitals, and actually, I was starting to feel better—with the exception of the continuous blood running down the side of my head. I looked down at the white undershirt and observed that it was soaked with my blood. Looking at the crate that still needed to be opened, I said to myself, "I have work to do."

Then I looked up to heaven and remembered the words of Jesus in the Bible. With that, I put my left hand on the wound where the blood was steadily flowing down and decided to ask the Lord to heal my head. "Lord, you said in your Word, *'Truly, truly, I say to you, whoever believes in me will do the works that I do; and greater works than these he will do. If you ask me anything in my name, I will do it.'*"[17]

I continued holding my hand to the side of my head and said, "So, I hold You to Your word that my head will be healed so that I can finish my work."

As I finished my simple prayer, the bleeding stopped and the side of my head was completely healed! All that remained was a

---

17 John 14:12, 14

little scar I could barely feel and a bloody t-shirt that used to be white. I looked up and said, "Thank you, Lord!" and went back to work. First, I took off the bloody t-shirt and put back on my camouflage shirt.

I never mentioned this incident to anyone unless I felt the need or was led to share it.

From that time, I would pray for friends who were sick or had some kind of pain, asking Jesus to heal them, mostly under my breath. Sometimes I would interrupt a conversation and pray for them to be healed. Jesus was listening to me and was answering those prayers. People would say later that they got better right after we talked.

Was it a coincidence? No! I knew it was Jesus.

It seems like I was always pushing the limits in everything I did, using "out-of-the-box" and unconventional ways. Most people who had been spiritually "neutered" or "spayed" wouldn't take the chances necessary for out-of-the-box thinking in everything.

I received four meritorious mast awards from commanding officers for outstanding work in military campaigns in my four-year tour of duty. I traded the processing paper work of one meritorious mast for a five-day R&R pass—the prejudiced gunnery sergeant agreed to it so he would not have to do the paperwork.

I took the R&R and caught a ride from Cherry Point, the Marine Air Wing, on a 5:00AM cargo flight to El Toro, California. It was a first-come, first-served ride to the Marine air base in Southern California. Upon arrival there, I caught another flight up to Travis Air Force Base in Northern California to my parent's home just outside of the base. On one of these trips home to California, I went to BJ's, a nightclub in Fairfield near the Travis base. My friend Jim worked at the door checking ID's. As we were talking one night, I noticed two girls across the dance floor sitting in a booth. To my surprise, it was Lorrie talking with her girlfriend. I could "see" that the girlfriend had a shadowy creature hanging over her. I went up to say hello to Lorrie and to see how she was doing.

"Oh, hi!" she responded, then looked over at her girlfriend for approval. I saw her "shine-him-on" response so wished her well and left her sitting there with her friend. It was much later that night I saw Lorrie alone and upset, so I went over to engage her in conversation. Come to find out, her girlfriend had left her stranded and took off with some guy. She was a little frantic about having had no way to get back home to Sacramento.

"You can spend the night at my parent's house. They have a bed on the enclosed patio," I offered. She accepted my invitation. We drove to my parents' home where everyone was already in bed asleep. I showed her where the bathroom was, and then tucking her into the sofa bed on the patio, I leaned over to kiss her softly on the forehead, "Goodnight!"

The next morning Lorrie was up early calling people, and she connected with her girlfriend for a ride back to Sacramento. She thanked me and my parents for their hospitality before heading back home.

It was also time for me to head back to Camp Lejuene. The five days had gone quickly, and college would soon be starting. When I arrived back at Lejuene, I discovered I was listed as AWOL (which is unauthorized leave), as the gunny sergeant had reported that he didn't know where I was. To clear things up, I produced the five-day R&R slip signed by the gunny himself. I had learned you must always be ready to produce proof to defend your actions from those who behave unrighteously.

I then started going to Coastal Carolina College a couple nights a week while also training at the Martial Arts Academy in the town of Jacksonville. For the sake of privacy and time for studying, I decided to move off base with a civilian roommate Butchie, a Puerto Rican from the Bronx, New York.

In the months that passed, I competed in karate tournaments in Raleigh, North Carolina. After one such tournament, the academy team decided to stay for the full-contact karate fights known as WKA, PKA, or IKA. This would be my second full-contact karate fight. The first was for a championship in Oakland, California, where I watched Benny (The Jet) Urquidez, at only 145 pounds demolish the 235-pound champion Phil Cornan.

At the start of the evening fights, the team found out the main event for the night was going to be cancelled because the challenger was ill. The promoter knew Bill, my instructor, and asked if he had any student that would be willing to fight a three-round fight. Bill had some of the top fighters on the east coast. He asked the team and everyone declined. Then, he turned to me with an inquiring look. I had that feeling—that nudging feel inside of me. I thought to myself, "Sure, why not? How hard could it be?" I honestly had no idea about full-contact fighting. Then I was told that this match originally had been for the new Amateur North Carolina Light Heavy Weight State Championship Title fight.

It was fight time, and I was the first to enter the ring. The crowd cheered as the opponent came out of the dressing room. Stepping into the ring, he straightened up, and as he did, he seemed to get taller and taller. He stood about 6'3", tall, dark, and very buffed.

The bell rang. As we fought, I remembered how "The Jet" kicked and moved. I now switched myself into a continuous nonstop flow of fighting, continually striking my opponent through each round or until we were stopped by the referee. The three rounds went quickly against the 6'3" giant-of-a-man.

The ring judges each gave a unanimous decision to me for the exhibition bout. This win brought my thoughts to the shepherd boy Bible story and how he took out an eight-foot giant named Goliath with God at his forefront.[18] This event was a pivotal turning point in dealing in the mystical events that would come my way.

I continued in WKA, PKA, and ISKA. Requests for me to fight as a welter weight came in from up and down the east coast of the

---

18 1 Samuel 17, story of David and Goliath

United States. During one fight, I heard the Voice say, "This is not your path but continue training." It was the desire of my heart to be one of the best. So, I decided to improve my fighting abilities by trying out for the U.S. Marine Corp boxing team at Camp Lejuene, and I was accepted on the base boxing team. I was training under Lt. Lombardi, developing my skills as I pushed the potential of this fighting sport to a whole new level. The words given to me at fifteen were still deeply implanted in my heart, *"Either Tibet and or the Himalayas would be my training grounds."* As I trained, I pondered the mystery of these words.

DECISION

It was a well-known fact that those who made it onto the U.S. Marine Corp Boxing Team (MC BT) soon became Olympic champions and/or professional world champions. I got to meet and train with Joe Lewis, the former full-contact World Karate Champion who was also training with the base boxing team and getting ready for his comeback from retirement.

It was at one of the local boxing events that I got to represent the MC base team. I walked into the fight venue to observe the ring. To my left, chairs and tables were set up around the ring. The people who were sitting and some standing around the ring had unique apparitions protruding in the air next to them. I continued walking through the building to the dressing rooms speaking with people along the way.

The sights I viewed where ghostly yet real in appearance. These ghostly influences were hanging above some of the people, especially the older boxers which I learned to distinguish. I began to realize that some of the ghostly affects where actually attached to the person whom they were over. Some of them resembled the person—or did the person resemble the figure, I wondered? These images also gave me insight into both the person's and the figure's personalities and character as the two they were one and the same.

The ghostly figures were making bets and wagers between themselves while the people they were connected to were sitting in conversation, or perhaps they were making wagers also. It was all so strange…I had never seen into mystical dimensions like this before. Then suddenly, one aberration pointed at me, shaking his head as the man followed suit. That was enough, and I wanted out of that place. As I headed to the dressing room, a man stopped me to shake hands and introduce himself. He seemed very nice. I found visual peace from the apparition when I got to the dressing room, as my mind was in deliberations over what I saw.

It was time for my boxing match, a three-round fight. Within the first minute, I knew that I could easily demolish the guy. Therefore, after I initially laid into him to get some respect, I took it easy; working on different styles without letting on that he was no match. The three rounds were finally over, and I was the unanimous winner. I was told that the crowd showed how much they loved a fighter by throwing money into the ring after each fight, and the ring, was filled with money. Our coach had someone collect and bring the money to me in the dressing room. After the evening's fights, the coach gathered the fighters together saying some of the old boxers wanted to meet us. They spoke to each of us but told me with great admiration, "You have what it takes! You are like a bull. We want to see you again…Yes, you have what it takes."

I was being distracted, looking in the back at the shadowy corner of the building next to the exit door. There was a dark, manly figure in the shadow, but I knew it was not a man. This figure seemed familiar, as if it seemed to be in charge of everything in the mystical realm. All the other creatures stayed clear of him unless they were summoned. The shadow figure observed everything while it followed my every movement with its head. Somehow I knew I would be seeing that shadow-of-a-man again.

That following Monday at training practice, the coach told me he wanted me to commit to full-time training with the boxing team and he would get me new orders for the Lejuene Boxing Team. Then, remembering what the Voice said to me, along with the glimpse of that shadow-of-a-man figure, along with my past dreams of the limo driver[19], I decided to end this career on the Lejuene Boxing Team. I continued to train in Martial Arts while remembering the prophecy of the Himalayas or Tibet. I continued to train in karate with some of the East Coast's Top National Martial Artists. The assistant instructor at the school was Carlos Fuentes, one of the best in the Kata divisions for open hand and with weapons. The light-weight fighting division belonged to Nick Burger. The Ancient Weapons Specialist in Kata and heavy-weight fighter was Lt. Tom Campbell from the U.S. Marines. I dominated the middle-weight division on the East Coast. The school closed during my second year as the instructor and students moved on.

I would like to give recognition to Carlos Fuentes who is now with the Lord after being killed while helping the sheriff's department bring down a drug cartel in Jacksonville, North Carolina. He was truly a friend and an extraordinary martial artist.

After the school closed, the Lord led me to Butch Velez III where I continued my training. Here I earned my black belt in Shi-To-Ryu Karate and Ju-jitsu under the American Goshin Budo & Kobudo Academy (AGK) in 1982, just after my tour of duty ended.

---

19 Chapter 3 Dead Reckoning "Black Limo and Driver"

Chapter Six

THE RETURN

AFTER MY TOUR OF duty had ended, I moved back to California after about 5 months. While going to college, I worked odd jobs and taught Shi-Toh-Ryu Karate-Do with Ju-Jitsu at Travis Air Force Base.

It was a beautiful, sunny December day, perfect for riding my motorcycle, and I decided to head to my mother's house for a little visit. Just as I walked through her front door, I heard my mom call out, "Ray, some girl just telephoned looking for you. She said that she saw you riding on that motorcycle and asked me how to get a hold of you."

"Did she leave a number?" I asked my mom, tossing my jacket on the living room chair. Reaching into her apron pocket, she pulled out a piece of paper with a number on it. I was very curious to know what girl was looking for me and quickly dialed her number.

"Hello? This is Lorrie speaking…" Recognizing her voice immediately I paused to catch myself from falling over.

"Oh! What a surprise…" I answered as calmly as I possibly could, though my excitement was hard to contain.

Lorrie came straight to the point, "I moved back to Fairfield just over a month ago and was looking for a friend. I remembered how you had taken care of me that night when my girlfriend took off and left me. I wanted to call and thank you again." She continued telling about the recent divorce between her mother and stepfather because of his alcoholism and other issues.

We agreed to meet at the picnic tables in a neighborhood park in 20 minutes. The anticipation of meeting her again had my heart jumping all over.

Approaching the park, I could see her from a distance and had to admire this beautiful young woman dressed so professionally. We were both excited at the reunion and greeted each other with hugs. For hours, we just sat and talked openly, examining one another, but my thoughts seemed to be everywhere at once: from my 10-item list to jumping off a bridge. Win or lose, I knew I could not bend or break those rules. As I shared these rules that guided me in looking for the right woman, the look on Lorrie's face stopped me. Her discerning look of beauty, staring deep into my eyes, just took my breath away, and I found it difficult to even remember my full list.

I can only describe what came next in baseball terms. I felt like a flash curve ball hit me straight between the eyes. As I recited the next point on my list of terms, she pitched her response right back at me by looking deep into my eyes with her own qualifying term, "So, hey! How about going to church with me…like this Sunday?"

I could have dropped to the ground with that, or go for a hit. *What should I do*, I pondered. I made a call, "Bring the bat up and bunt the curve ball!" I was not sure if I swung at it I would actually make a hit, but at least I could make the run to first base. I decided to take her question to me as a "Yes!" to my list of terms. For the rest of the evening, we both just relaxed, knowing we had satisfied the values we lived by.

Watching the sunset—sitting at first base together—I accepted her invitation.

I picked her up on Sunday, and together we went to her church in Vacaville, California. It was called Vaca Valley Christian Life Center (VVCLC) at the time in January 1983 and was led by Pastor Jerry Hannon. In a silent prayer during the service, I asked God, "So, what do you say about this place?" I heard him say "It is a good place." That was all I needed to hear.

Lorrie was first introduced to this church by her roommate's daycare provider whom everyone called "Aunt Patty." From the first day I met her, I watched as she spoke wisdom and grace into the lives of people going through trials of life. I saw her living the words of Jesus:

> *A new commandment I give to you, that you love one another: just as I have loved you, you also are to love one another.* (John 13:34)

Aunt Patty was a lighthouse guiding people into safe ports of harbor. She was a testimony of Jesus' love to me and scores of people.

Within two years, Lorrie and I got married at that same church. Over time, we had three sons: our first Jacob followed by Joshua 13 months afterwards, and then Josiah, the tailgater seven years later. I know our sons arrived just the way I had made the request of God as a young child.

RESENTMENT

The world's ways began to harden me on some things, and after God had granted my request for all I wanted in a wife, I almost blew it in our relationship. I learned that if you harden your heart, you could miss out on life and your true love. There are times in relationships where situations will present an opportunity to be hurt and offended with one another. This would happen with us every so often. When I asked the Lord about it, He showed me what the root cause was in my life. He took me back to that evening at the nightclub when I met Lorrie again a few years after high school; I had felt like she with her girlfriend were rejecting me. I realized since that time, I had held resentment against my wife and it reflected in the way I treated her for years. Because of this, she was growing to hate me in that season. It took years to unlearn these patterns, to forgive each other, and transform the way we had been relating to one another with its harmful effects on our relationship. It was Lorrie's tenacious love and her determination to not give up on our marriage that finally broke the bitterness in me. Lorrie is a person who believes and holds to God's Word no matter what the situation. We are not perfect by any means, but we have exchanged ungodly patterns for relating to one another in love.

Steadfastness is a part of love, and love will prevail if we are willing to change and not harden our hearts. In order to avoid traveling such a difficult road in your own personal relationships, I urge you to ask the Lord to show you if there is any bitterness you are harboring in your heart. I know this: if we are willing to unharden our hearts and transform the way we think and do, the desires of our hearts will be fulfilled.

Lorrie and I have celebrated 30 years of marriage, and our oldest son Jacob just got married. What a testimony of God's grace transforming our hearts and lives.

Take a moment right now to think back on the pure, innocent desires of your heart that had no ulterior motives—just the innocence of your heart. Write these down in the "Notes" section at the end of this book. As you reflect back to that time, I believe you will see something very special. Know that God is working with you to see that through.

By the way, Lorrie's mother Chris remarried George—a great stepfather and grandfather for her family. I myself continually have to check my own heart, for hardness wants to creep back in.

THE BOYS

It was at our son Jacob's birth that the Lord very simply told me, "Jacob will lead many people." He was a strong-willed and joyous child, walking at the age of ten months. Jacob earned his Bachelor's of Science in Biology from Sonoma University. His wife Cara has presently graduated from Bethel School of Supernatural, working on her ministry calling.

At his birth, Joshua had a spirit that I had never seen on a person before. This spirit had the might of Samson and the heart of Moses' aid Joshua. The Lord spoke to my heart about him and said, "He and his brother will be a team."

At Josiah's birth, I received no specific prophetic word with the exception of his name. When he was about 8 years of age, however, God spoke to me about Josiah through some spiritual experiences and supernatural encounters.

I was excited to finally be able to meet Lorrie's natural father, Clarence. Lorrie's Great Aunt Goldie called and invited us to come over to her house so we could be with her father who was in town that week. He expressed his desire to see his grandsons, our boys. Clarence and I stepped outside of the house away from all the relatives to spend some personal time together, just getting to know each other. His final words to me really made a strong impression that I will never forget: "Please…take care of my daughter."

A few years after that incident, I had a heavenly vision while attending a MorningStar Ministries pastor's and leader's conference. The Lord spoke clearly to me about my son: "Josiah will lead your sons and others. The things you will not do, he will do. You are to pave a road for him."

Then, instantly, I was translated. Having a machete in my right hand, I was swinging it through the jungle, paving a path as others were following behind me. Then as I looked behind me to check on the others, I could see a small road that had been created as I cleared the path. As I continued cutting my way through the jungle, I looked a second time behind me, but now there was a two-way road. I turned forward and continued hacking away in a determined, declarative prayer: "I will pave a highway for my son, Lord." As I spoke this out, I was no longer in the heavenly realm, but my hand was still swinging as if I was cutting through the jungle with a machete.

In that moment, I knew it was necessary to transform my way of thinking. I once read how the Wright brothers tried to prove their theory of flight by using a theory that turned out to have major flaws. As they pursued their objective with diligence and with all of their heart, they eventually saw the flaw, corrected it, and the rest is history. I knew I must pursue what God had just showed me in the same way.

In history, we see that before the realization of a dream, there first must be a personal breakthrough, and then a corporate breakthrough comes. These often come in evolutionary steps. When an individual or team of people take steps through the door seeking revelation, it creates a grace or an anointing for breakthrough on a personal level and then on a corporate level. From there, it brings a global release. We see examples of this through the brilliance of such people as Marie Curie, Albert Einstein, and Rosa Parks, to name a few. Just as God showed me in the vision that hacking my way through the jungle created a path which became a road which morphed into a two-way highway and eventually a major thoroughfare which others could follow, so too a personal-to-corporate breakthrough will only come through helping and heavily depending upon one another.

This is a paradox of unparalleled measure for the past, the present, and revelations of the future—in both the natural and unseen realms. It has to be first spiritually seen, and then it will manifest in the natural and be released. It is best understood to many from the scientific community to the religious community in two Scriptures:

> *The secret things belong to the Lord our God, but the things that are revealed belong to us and to our children forever."* (Deuteronomy 29:29)

> *It is the glory of God to conceal things, but the glory of kings is to search things out.* (Proverbs 25:2)

ENTREPRENEUR

Gifts and abilities have come with God's favor as Lorrie and I have opened our businesses over the years. We learned to take steps that seemed to be unrealistic in the natural and were expanded beyond measure as God's favor brought with it knowledge and wisdom.

My Uncle Adolph taught me about being a businessman. He owned a commercial block in the city of Chicago, and yet, started from nothing. I once called him asking to borrow $10,000 dollars.

"I don't have that kind of money, Ray," he said. "Sorry!"

"Oh…" I was clearly disappointed. *There go my dreams*, I was thinking to myself. Without the money, my business dream was over.

"Well, thanks anyway, Uncle Adolph…" My mind was in a free-fall, completely at a loss as to how to get such a substantial amount of money.

I was about to hang up when my uncle blurted out, "Hey Ray! Wait! What is the *minimum* amount you need to get started? When you figure that out, let me know." Then I heard "click" on the other end of the line as we disconnected.

But the click ignited a spark of hope in me…right then, right there. I had just learned a new way of looking at things. I needed to change my business mindset.

A few days went by as I was estimating the equipment needed for procurement to get started. After thoroughly researching my minimal startup needs, I called Uncle Adolph back.

"I will need $2,000 dollars to start my business," I reported. My uncle sent me the money, and I agreed to repay him over the next two years. This was our first business, and we repaid my uncle within a year.

Lorrie and I started opening numerous businesses over the next ten years, ranging from hair salons and tanning beds to a seasonal apparel boutique that carried gold jewelry and precious stones. Over time we diversified into the food industry and opened a yogurt shop.

In all of these experiences through these years, I learned the deeper meaning of the Hebrew word *emunah,* which in English is translated "believe." This word means much more than just "believe," however; it is also "faith" joined with believing who God says we are and who are to become. True *emunah* is a person continuing to trust God and that what He says will happen—*will* happen. We held to *emunah* through many difficult times. We have come to believe—and have faith—that God's Word never fails.

It was during one of the rough times in business that we had to close the doors to all but one of our businesses due to a theft incident by one of our employees. We were praying to the Lord for His help lest we would have to close the doors on the primary business as well.

Every day I went to work knowing that the business had to make at least $1,400 by the end of that day or the doors would be closed. One day, a little after 5:10 PM and with less than an hour until closing, there was less than $400 in the till. We prayed again, "Lord, we need help!" as Lorrie got up from her chair to finish her last hair client for the day.

She turned and said to me, "Let's close up and go home when I am done."

"The Lord didn't carry us this far," I responded, "Just to drop us. No, we will stay until 6:00 PM normal closing time."

Within a few minutes, the phone rang.

"Hi, I know it is late notice, but would it be possible for my girlfriend and I to have our hair and nails done right away?" she inquired.

"Come on over!" I responded, excited at this quick answer to prayer.

The Return

The two new customers arrived just ten minutes before closing. As they waited between Lorrie's services, I sold one of them 14k-gold bracelets. I happened to notice that the lady who paid for everything had a gold necklace with a devil head pendant on it. I felt I had to do something without shutting her down. I could sense the presence of God pursuing her with His love. I reached into the jewelry case and pulled out a beautiful 14K-gold piece depicting Christ ascending and I could not help but observe her eyes as I handled it.

Extending the beautiful piece of jewelry towards her I said, "Here...please accept this as a gift from me." Her eyes widened in excitement as she stared after the gold piece transferring from my hands to hers.

"May I place it on you?" I offered, unlatching the gold necklace. She turned around, allowing me to drape it around her neck as she fingered it tenderly.

Turning around to admire it in the salon mirror she said, "It's just beautiful...so beautiful, thank you!"

I stated, "You will remove the devil head one day as I cannot remove it. You will remove it one day when you are ready. Know that God has you in His hands and HE loves you. The ladies said good night as they left at 9:45PM. The *Lord* had delivered the money as promised being exactly what was needed to stay open. We thanked God. I have not seen the woman or her friend since but was told by Lorrie and others that she came in a few times looking for me. Hear these words: God not only helps in time of need, but He touches others if you are willing to take a step of *emunah*.

During these rough times, Vaca Valley Christian Life Center, our home church, bought some land and was making plans to build a school along with a gymnasium in which services would be held. I saw a shift coming and felt it was time to start looking for a new career. I began working at Travis AFB with the Civil

Engineering Repair Maintenance Inspect Team (CERMIT), and in a short time, I again earned letters of recommendation for outstanding work. It was after traveling for work 265 days out of the first year that I started doing correspondent college classes which took a little over two years to complete. During this time, we bought a move-up home the same time the church moved into the newly built school structure. It seemed to me that every time the church increased, so did we and vice versa. Coincidence or not?

In 1999, Daniel McCollam (Dan) came to VVCLC to minister and was asked to become the associate pastor to Dave Crone who was now the senior pastor. Dan brought this crazy laughter to the church that was imparted to him through a Rodney Howard Brown meeting in Louisville, Kentucky, in 1994. It was one Sunday as Dan was praying for people that Lorrie got hit/imparted with that spirit of laughter and joy mentioned in Psalm 126 and Nehemiah 8:10. It was this laughter that helped bring us through the tough times. On many occasions, you could see this gift from God given to Lorrie bring down strongholds, offending the spirit of religion and its relatives while bringing great healings and release:

Peace I leave with you; my peace I give to you. Not as the world gives do I give to you. Let not your hearts be troubled, neither let them be afraid. (John 14:27)

The years went by as Lorrie's ability to spiritually know and feel increased. Our spiritual gifts intensified as we both learned to work together as a team. This was a fulfilled desire of our hearts. The desires of our hearts are special gifts given to us all. I want you to take the next seven days—before each meal and before you go to bed—to ask the *Lord* about the desire of your heart that you have requested. Keep a pencil and paper close by even when you go to bed to write down what the Lord tells you.

Lord Jesus, I ask You to show them what they might have missed and to reveal the desires of their hearts as it is requested of You. I ask that the pure innocent desires that have not been released be released now with Your love, peace, and joy. May they, and all of whom they come in contact with, be enlightened by who You are, Jesus. I Thank You for hearing and allowing me to release this request over them. In Your name. Amen.

Chapter Seven

GET READY

IN THE BEGINNING CHAPTER of this book, I talked about sound being similar to light as it resonates through space, time, and matter. For your own further study, I highly recommend that you read Dan McCollam books on the physics of sound and how it affects matter, *God Vibrations: the Power of Sound*. The findings will transform the way you think.

In the continuing research throughout history I find simple questions answered through breakthroughs that take us back to the beginning. The things of scientific knowledge that we are taught since grade school develop through further education, but where did it start? Let's consider that creative ideas come from another source other than thought processing. They often originate from the spiritual realm through:
- A dream,
- A vision,
- A revelation, i.e., a word of knowledge from the Holy Spirit

Here are two scientists who received such revelatory ideas leading the way to their discoveries. Thomas Edison saw lightning and began to explore the potential of its power, thus leading the way to discovering how to utilize electricity in everyday life. Because of this revelation and through future creative ideas and inventions, power sources bring electricity into every home and business for a multitude of uses. Computer technology, which has advanced our society beyond our wildest imaginations, was only made possible through electricity.

Albert Einstein, with his developments of relativity $E=Mc^2$, stated in his letters to a colleague that he "saw it." He went on to say, "If it is not true, God must have been pulling my leg." Such "ideas" come from a revelatory vision; it is through actually "seeing" it that our mind becomes transformed, allowing for the release of words of knowledge from the Holy Spirit.[20] Whether you believe in God or not, the Holy Spirit checks everyone's heart and the intent of their desires. It is God's Word to us that gives us the desires of the heart.[21] Remember this, "If you can see it, you can have it."[22] This has been constant since the beginning of time for breakthrough and advancement—so I say go after it. I have often wondered why more Christians are not involved as scientists since revelations are given to them. I have found most scientists are, in fact, Christians. Those who are not, I have learned that someone close to them—a parent, spouse, or friend—prays for them regularly so that they receive scientific breakthroughs through dreams and visions. There is a continuing revelation, as the advancement of technology unfolds true awareness in the scientific community, that there is a Creator of this ever-expanding universe.

Are you ready for the next metamorphosis?

I was. So, I took college courses and decided to change careers by going into real estate financing. I was preparing for the next changes in my life, knowing God's favor and wisdom always follow. At the same time, during this transition in my life in 1997, the sanctuary of my church, Vaca Valley Christian Life Center,[23] was also being built. On the vacant lot next to its school facility, the leaders did a prophetic act together by

---

20 Romans 12:2

21 Psalm 37:4.

22 Deuteronomy 29:29. God, our God, will take care of the hidden things but the revealed things are our business. It's up to us and our children to attend to all the terms in this Revelation. (Message)

23 Presently named "The Mission" in Vacaville, California.

putting precious stones into the concrete foundation as it was being poured.[24]

Simultaneously, Lorrie and I bought a lot to build a home, yet we had no money to do this. It was a desire of my heart to give my boys and Lorrie the very best. My sons became laborers in the effort of building our home, helping to carry the building materials up the hill for the contractor during its construction. The boys and I planted a mini vineyard on the hillside of the backyard of both wine and table grapes. There, we had an alcove cut into the hillside where I would spend time talking with the Lord as I pruned the vines. Such lessons He gave me.

In 1998, I was working in my vineyard when I heard the Voice which had spoken ever so clear, audible, and loud to me in the 60s. It was in the same tone that told me, "Go play!" This time it said simply, "Get ready!"

"GET READY!"

Over time I began to realize God's time is not our time—it could be in the present or perhaps 40 years from now, as with Moses in the desert. I started preparing the best way I knew how by re-reading the Bible from cover to cover a little each day. As I did, I was looking for keys, following the leading of the Holy Spirit in reading His Word as I felt Him nudging me, whether it was convenient or not.

It was during this time Lorrie felt led to give me a book that she thought would help. It was called, *The Quest*, by Rick Joyner.[25] This book pole-vaulted me higher in searching out the prophetic gifts. I found MorningStar Ministries was made up of many types of prophets, seers, hearers, and others enabled with revelatory

---

[24] Dave Crone addresses more detail about this in his book, *Decisions That Define Us*.

[25] *The Final Quest* by Rick Joyner was published in March 1996. MorningStar Publications and Ministries, www.morningstarministries.org

Spirit-gifts. It sparked a hunger in me to pursue more fully the gifts God had given me.

> *To one is given through the Spirit the utterance of wisdom, and to another the utterance of knowledge according to the same Spirit, **9** to another faith by the same Spirit, to another gifts of healing by the one Spirit, **10** to another the working of miracles, to another prophecy, to another the ability to distinguish between spirits, to another various kinds of tongues, to another the interpretation of tongues. **11** All these are empowered by one and the same Spirit, who apportions to each one individually as he wills.* (1Corinthians 12: 8-11).

I came to realize that there were resources that would help me mature in how to walk in the gifts of the Holy Spirit. I began reading many of the books available through MorningStar Ministries and others. These books gave testimonies with practical insight of those who walked in these revelatory Spirit-abilities.

THE JOURNEY BEGINS

Vaca Valley Christian Life Center brought in a new worship leader, Michael Schuler, in 2000. Michael had an anointing for opening portals into the heavenly realm where Heaven and Earth connected. In worship, I often saw angels ascending and descending where we gathered. This was the first time I was caught up in the heavenly realm by the sound of corporate worship music. It was in one of those heavenly encounters that the weight of God's glory was so intense I dropped to my knees, literally ripping a hole in my jeans. Inclusive of this time period our youngest son, Josiah, age 8, announced to us that he wanted to be baptized. We all joined him in the baptism.

The Sunday service started with a total of nine people being baptized. There was something magnetized in the atmosphere that was felt by many. The worship ended and just seemed to flow uninterrupted into the message.

I was in a vision at the time the sermon began, kneeling down on one knee with my head bowed. I could see the outlined face of the Lord in full detail. His face took on many appearances, but still with the same face. All the nationalities of the world seemed to shine on His face.

Seeing myself in the natural, I was actually physically standing, observing all of this. Instantly there appeared on my left arm a shield and in my right hand there was a sword. As I observed the sword, it looked like a regular sword. Then as I gazed at it, I was amazed as a puff of smoke rose from the sword. Then it suddenly became fully engulfed in a small flame. It was a new release.

I continued observing myself kneeling down on one knee. I began to physically step back further and further as the flame of the sword grew brighter and more intense. The further back I stepped, the more the flame would erupt. Now I was no longer an observer watching myself with the sword; I was actually holding the sword with the tip touching the ground, with the shield on my arm, and the flame a constant consuming fire. I could hear the Voice saying: *These will be your protection, you will learn to use them and they will grow.*

As I heard His voice, I realized this was a set of instructions for me saying, "It is not by what we can do in our own strength, but it is by the Spirit we succeed."

As I continued to watch the vision unfold, my wife Lorrie touched my hand. She was on one knee, and I could see that she was dressed in armor from the neck down. Then both of our hands were on the sword hilt—my right hand and her left hand—as the flames that engulfed the sword grew with a great intensity, illuminating the space around both of us. My thoughts went to the scripture in Ephesians 6 about putting on the whole armor of God and using the shield of faith to extinguish the fiery darts of the enemy. The sword, which is the Word of God, reminded me of the significance to always stay in prayer.

Towards the end of the sermon, David Crone asked all those with "little or no faith" to step forward. A minute later, he asked those with faith to step forward to stand as a shield of faith around those in need. I, among many others, stepped forward and stood around them as a shield of prayer for those in need.

While in this shield position, I saw something like a light grey yet solid cloud around those who stepped forward. Everything else was obscured in the natural. I then heard the Voice say, "Turn around." I tried to ignore the Voice, but it was persistent. With an even deeper tone, it said again, "Turn around!" With everyone facing forward and my natural eyes still closed, I physically turned around. It was then that I saw huge angels on each side of me with swords and shields in their hands, a pure white wrap around their bodies, and golden sashes around their waists. Scanning them from head-to-toe and looking all around, I realized I was no taller than their ankles. The angel to my right spoke these words to me: "You will grow like us. Nothing will get past you, no matter how big it is, unless you allow it."

In that moment, I thought to myself, *I am like an ant among the giants,* as I looked from the top of the angel's head to the ankles. I looked behind me and saw the light grey cloud of a shield covering the people. The angel spoke again looking directly at me, "Your direction is this way," and then turned his head towards the direction that the other angels were looking. As I opened my eyes, I heard the angel say, "For now." I was looking with my eyes open in the natural now and seeing the angels along with the shield of protection they were providing as they surrounded all the people from behind.

The people were now being released by David to return back to their seats.

There on the platform steps during this encounter lay envelopes for charitable donations with amounts ranging from ten dollars to five hundred dollars. I walked over intending to pick up a hundred dollar envelope to give a charitable contribution. Just as I reached for the $100 dollar envelope, my natural vision became incapacitated and I could see nothing except the $10, $20, and $500 dollar envelopes. I turned my head from side to side trying to see the steps, but to no avail. My vision was obscured of everything except for these three envelopes on the steps. Rubbing my eyes, looking away for a moment, and then turning back again, I was still only able to view the same items on the altar steps. I thought to myself, *the $10 and $20 dollar amounts are no big deal for a charitable donation. I wanted to do more!* I knew that a $100 hundred donation would be a little stretch, but a $500 donation was a big sacrifice and way more than I could afford. I said, "Lord, I put my trust in you!" and quickly grabbed the $500 envelope. I stepped out in faith to believe that the Lord clearly showed what He wanted me to donate to this charity, even though I knew it was a huge sacrifice for us. This was a strengthening of my faith as I felt the shield on my arm got broader and lighter. In time, I began to realize it was not a weight put upon me, but increased strength.

This was also the day I began writing down the encounters of dreams, visions, and trances I had experienced. I felt this was an important act for me as stated in Habakkuk 2:2:

Write the vision; make it plain on tablets, so he may run who reads it.

As God gives you revelatory words, write them down no matter how small they seem. What you are receiving from Him will be keys for you, His prophetic decree. Recording His words to you is a way to honor what He gives you.

The months passed. I was told in a dream to go to MorningStar Ministries. I went to the MorningStar website and researched the upcoming conferences over the next few months. I viewed the ad for a five-day Pastors and Leadership Advance and felt nudged by the Holy Spirit about this conference.

The turning points in our lives come with opportunity as a step. But, if you don't take the step, you run the risk of becoming complacent. I wasn't asked if I was financially ready to give such a large donation to this charity on that day, and clearly I was not. I only knew it would be a forward advancement of perpetual motion.

I see these opportunities as Thomas Jefferson once said:

I have sworn, upon the altar of God, eternal hostility against every form of tyranny over the mind of man.[26]

I put this concept into my own words which I firmly believe:
The fear that interferes with a calling of God is tyranny of the mind.

---

26 Thomas Jefferson stated to Dr. Benjamin Rush, September 23, 1800 and others.

Chapter Eight

MORAVIAN FALLS

I WAS REALLY HOPING to have a leader with me, so I asked Michael Schuler, the worship leader at Vaca Valley Christian Life Center at that time, to join me in going to the MorningStar conference. He accepted. When we arrived, there were high levels of prophetic authority from the MorningStar body. Having never been in a body of Christians with such a natural prophetic emancipation, I found the environment an experience of personal release.

There were various speakers at the conference, but two in particular stood out. There was an elderly man with the head of a bald eagle, and another man who was black with a white beard which made him appear quite discerning and very distinguished. He resembled the actor, James Baskett, from the 1946 movie, *Song of the South*. The Morningstar worship team consisted of Leonard Jones, Suzie Wills, and others. During the worship, I was taken into the very presence of the Lord. I was nearly blinded as I entered the heavenly realm right into His throne room—I was no longer in the conference. Everything turned bright and white as the sound being released was precise and perfect with a uniqueness that penetrated deep into a person. It was drawing me deeper into the realm; my inner being or soul could feel my spirit singing.

GLORY

It was glorious in all its brightness with a serenity that was a sanctification of beauty, peace, and joy without measure. The band was dressed in pure white garments that were getting whiter and whiter as they continued singing, dancing, and giving their praise to Him. I could see the music coming from their hearts, souls, and their very essence as it was released. The ambiance was getting brighter. They began to blend with the elements of the throne room that was surrounding them.

Then suddenly things became slightly grey. I became a bit concerned at this change as I had not left the heavenly realm. Then I heard this:

This veil is for your protection.

I could still see the worship team as the vision escalated in brightness, extending into the heavenly glory. Then, for a fraction of a second, I saw the bottom of the Throne along with what looked like the foot of a man so radiant; it would have blinded me without the veil. I had to look away from the radiance of the light and was now only able to hear the praising sound of worship, for all I could see was the radiance protruding out in waves of light similar to heat waves.

I did not want to leave that place. As I opened my eyes, all I could see in the natural was brightness of pure, heavenly whiteness. When I could finally see more clearly, I sat down to process what just happened in the heavenly realm…or had the heavenly realm come to earth like in the transfiguration of Mark 9:2?

> *And after six days Jesus took with him Peter and James and John, and led them up a high mountain by themselves. And he was transfigured before them, and his clothes became radiant, intensely white, as no one on earth could bleach them. (Mark 9:2)*

The music ended shortly, and Rick Joyner introduced the bald eagle-looking man as "the great-grandfather of the prophetic, Prophet Bob Jones." After the meeting, the black man I had noticed came up and introduced himself to me. As I shook his hand, our connection sent a staggering jolt into my body, and he had to hold tightly onto my hand to keep me upright. Right then he took me over to introduce me to Bob Jones saying, "You need to meet him…" There was an immediate surge of power as we shook hands together that shot through Bob's hand into mine, greater than the current I felt when I accidently cut into a live 440 circuit as an electrician. Right then, someone else came up to talk with Bob, and I sat on the floor right behind them, trying to regain some kind of composure from the experience with the two men I had just "connected" with.

This experience was followed by an increase of many more dreams, visions, and encounters that I realized were a direct impartation from those two gentlemen. In this new release, I could actually go into a global-type trance or vision, observing what other prophetic people were doing, and I believed I was even communicating with a few of them. Some had no idea where they were or if it was real. The impartations came with greater authority, increased power of the abilities, as well as an increase of knowledge.

That brought me to words of wisdom from my dad, Raymond, as lined up from his life experiences:

God first, always. (1st Commandment)

Take care of your health, second. What if something happens to you because you don't take care of yourself physically? Who is going to take care of your family? (1Corinthians 6:20)

Take care of your family. Resolve any issues before you do anything else? (Luke 6:41, 12:57-59)

Help those in need when you can. (Luke 6:34-36, James 1:22)

Always give a 110% at work and in whatever you do. It doesn't matter what everyone else does. (1Peter 2:13-17)

Take care of my grandchildren.

I love you and God bless you.

I kept coming back to other Morningstar conferences with my wife and oldest son from 2002 through 2004. Returning to those conferences became markers and beacons for the calling.

On one of these return trips, I had arrived by plane into the Charlotte International Airport, rented a car, and drove to the hotel. I got up early the next morning to go register at the conference. The doors were unlocked, so I entered through the front door of the building. About 10 feet directly in front of me was a blond-headed lady sitting behind the registration table. As I approached her table, she blurted out loudly (to her own astonishment), "You will lead the prophetic..." paused, and then continued, "and you will have authority over the prophetic."

I turned around to look behind me to see whom she might be speaking to, but there was no other person there except another working at the registration table. With a look of bewilderment she said, "I don't know why I said that to you. I don't know where that came from." As she finished processing my registration, she looked up at me and declared, "Yes, you do hear the voice of the Lord, and you have authority."

As she handed me the name badge for the conference, she said, "I am not quite sure about the full meaning of the word 'authority,'" but I knew this was an affirming word from God. All that day I pondered "You will lead the prophetic..."

It was at another MorningStar conference that Lorrie's prophetic gifts began to be unveiled. She was beginning to understand that her spiritual experiences as a child were not childhood folly but the result of a genuine gift of the Spirit that was always there. At this realization, Lorrie's whole countenance changed with such pleasure as she enthusiastically exercised her gifts. This started a chain of events that connected prophetic decrees as they were released at our home church.

On Labor Day weekend, August 2003, we had a three-day conference with Cleddie Keith. This man is a bold straight-shooter with a no-holds-barred approach when it came to speaking words of knowledge he received. His prophetic declarations were unmatched by those I had heard up to that time. It was during the middle of one of the sessions that Cleddie stopped his teaching at the podium and looked directly at me. He turned his body completely towards me, and in his loud and rough, yet sincere, appeal shouted, "What are you waiting for?"

He then continued as he focused his attention on me, "The things you are going to do, the people you will reach, and touch... what are you waiting for? What are you waiting for?"

Then he turned back to finish the sermon about the Hebrew word, *tehilah,* meaning, spontaneous worship, from Psalm 22. As Cleddie finished, again, he stopped everything, turned to Lorrie, and speaking directly to her said, "Quit trying to second guess what the Lord is doing. You are smart, but the Lord is smarter, so quit trying to second-guess Him. You need to support what the Lord is going to do through your husband..." He went on to say that he has seen marriages destroyed because the wife does not support what the Lord has called the husband to do. "Get up and dance with him...do things with him, because I don't want to see this happen with you."

What came next in less than a year released more of the declaration.

DIVINE APPOINTMENTS AT MORNINGSTAR

In April 2004, I attended another MorningStar conference in Charlotte, North Carolina. At 4:01 Sunday morning, I was awakened by the Lord. My mind went directly to the events earlier that day at the conference. I knew I needed to write them down when I got up. The events were guideposts for the calling that lay before me. It started with Lorrie and me seeking the location of the Garr Auditorium at the close of the afternoon session. The auditorium was the venue where author Steve Thompson would be sharing about the ministry of "The 21st Century Apostle Alfred Garr" who moved in signs and wonders during the 1940s. Unable to find the venue on the map or GPS, I went up to Steve to ask him how to get to the Garr Auditorium.

That next second Steve called his assistant Jim over to us, with an introduction, and asked Jim to show us. Jim was also part of the senior prophetic team of Morningstar. I asked where the auditorium was as I pulled out a small map of Charlotte. Jim took me over to a huge map that hung on the back wall next to the exit door of the building as Lorrie went to wait outside.

There were three ladies sitting next to where Jim and Steve had been sitting. These three ladies called Jim over to them as we were looking at the big map for directions. I was looking at the map waiting for Jim to return. A moment later, he returned and said to me, "Those ladies have a word for you if you would like to hear it." I responded, "Yes, I would."

Jim and I went over to the ladies who introduced themselves to me, saying they had been observing me. "Here, have a seat," they offered me. I was a little unsure about being under their microscope, yet excited at the same time. The ladies prayed before moving into words of knowledge.

The first word released was a question, "Do you know who Cesar Chavez is and what he did?" I looked at them and replied, "No, I don't."

Then, one of the ladies, Kiela, with long straight dark hair said to me, "You need to find out who he was and what he did." Then the ladies all together began to release words to me like a fountain of fresh water, and I drank as quickly as possible, trying to keep it from overflowing. Here are words I received that day.

> (1) You have a role as a leader much like Cesar Chavez was for the Hispanic people. You are a protector—the leader for the common man. It is similar to the role of a labor union organizer.

She paused as Jim jumped in saying, "I have a word…" as he spoke.

(2) I see you as a businessman. You are a networker with the ability to bring people together connecting one to another. These people would not have connected without you being the hub. You will be leading and connecting everyone together just as a hub that connects computers and components.

As they finished, Ginger, with her blonde hair and wide-open eyes full of excitement, spoke.

(3) She first confirmed what Jim said, coming into agreement with him. Then she agreed with Kiela, as she had seen those things too.

Last was Priscilla, a very tall young woman with curly dark hair and a look that said, "I don't play around… listen to what I have to say! It is for your benefit that I speak!" And she delivered her word with great authority in her voice.

(4) She began with my history of the sandbox when I was a child and the promise I made to God because of that. She went into great detail and got my full attention. The reading was so impacting as she reiterated the things that changed my life as a child along with the promise that I swore. This had been a secret until that moment. This reached deeply into me, opening my heart as she revealed the "sandbox story" and even more. [27]

While she was reading my mail, my leg began to bounce up and down in the chair like it was a basketball. The Spirit intensified as

---

[27] Chapter 3

my body began to bounce up and down as though being dribbled down a basketball court from the manifestation of the Actual presence.

> Priscilla continued, "God has protected you and your heart and has molded it. He continues to protect it. You are a protector; you have the leadership of speech to guide men." As she paused for a moment, she said that she wasn't sure if it was for men only. She persisted with that same comment three times. Then said, "I believe it may be for women also. You are heavily anointed by the Lord for what He has for you to do. The Lord is preparing you now; He is bringing you out now, and in times, as it is almost your time. You have the heart for people, giving protection for them and over them."

The Holy Spirit's presence increased as they spoke the words, and I became drained, but empowered, at the same time.

Ginger added more:

> (5) "I saw all the things that others saw. We can all see what the Lord has done for you and all that you are going to do. You can't even begin to see it or understand now, but you will. You have now and will have the arms of His strength."

Jim again:

> (6) "I see a waterfall, and you are in it. You are being protected by the Lord; you cannot be touched there. It is your and the Lord's place; you go there to get away a lot. It is the Lord's place for He molds your heart there and protects it. You will be a networker."

Priscilla:

(7) "You will help; you will protect; you will lead; and you will connect others." They all said in one accord, "You have a wild heart."

They all prayed in agreement for me and with me for the Lord's will and for standing upright with strength. At that moment, I felt my body straighten up as my heart grew stronger, and my back aligned while lifting in length as if I was growing at that moment.

They continued to stare at me sitting there. Then one of them asked if I had come alone to the conference.

"My wife is here with me," I replied.

"We'd like to see her," they told me.

"She's outside waiting for me..." With that, Jim went outside to get Lorrie and bring her over to where we were sitting. They said to Lorrie, "I wish you had heard what was spoken over your husband." They were observing her and then decided to speak with her in private.

(8) These are the last few words spoken by them; "You have the anointing of Benjamin of the 12 tribes." This was repeated three times. I looked up the blessing of Benjamin.

Benjamin is a wolf that prowls. He devours his enemies in the morning and in the evening he divides the plunder. (Genesis 49:27)

Over time, I have found this word to be a big part of my calling.

GARR AUDITORIUM

When they had finished, we drove to Garr Auditorium. I was really affected by the area where the venue was located—in the slums of Charlotte in much need of restoration. I could see angels standing and waiting in the unseen realm over wells and portals for what awaited this area of the city. I don't know if it was emotions or the Spirit touching me in regards to that place. It was a lot to see, hear, and carry back home to California as I began to understand the calling of my seer gift more and more.

Everything a seer receives he is responsible to declare in a way that will build up and edify.

The conference was so profound that Lorrie and I brought our oldest son Jacob to the continuation of this prophetic conference that June. It was at this conference Jacob got touched by the finger of God. Here at the conference, I saw Keila and asked if she remembered me. She responded, "I remember you…the five-fold of Benjamin. Yes…you have the five-fold of Benjamin." Those words reached a deep place in me, pulling on the reason for my existence.

Jacob was like a sponge soaking everything up, leaving nothing, and searching for more. His gifting into dreams and visions opened up with a greater clarity and understanding. Jacob started recording in his own journal what he receives, as it protects and guides him. I have watched him help others who are ignored or shunned by society with his gifted abilities.

Chapter Nine

EPIPHANY

SOMETIMES WE SEERS ARE so caught up in the unseen we miss the obvious. At a bookstore one day, Lorrie saw the book *Wild at Heart* by John Eldridge with a picture on the cover of a man jumping across a mountain raven in shorts. She knew I would enjoy it as a Christmas gift. In the book was a new book marker that looked like a hundred dollar bill and which would later become significant. I was so inspired by the book that after reading it, I signed up for the men's boot camp that John Eldridge and his team host twice a year. With the acceptance to the boot camp in Colorado, my heart jumped with such fire as anticipation grew. The experience reached into the very essence of the way a man is designed to be and act.

After returning from the boot camp, I tried hard to interpret what a retreat of this kind would do for those desiring to go deeper in strength, perseverance, and the release of fear while walking on a ledge of faith that is genuine and that only going and doing will release. Each person at this retreat had a limit of how far they would let their faith take them. Those who dared to trust pole-vaulted into new levels that words cannot express. This was an investment in my future of things that were going to be released in the call of a seer. It is like building your stock portfolio with guaranteed dividends. These kinds of exercises are like fires reignited with restoration in every aspect of life's journey. The impossible becomes possible.

Upon my return from the *Wild at Heart* retreat, I was sitting in Starbucks one morning, reading another book. A person waiting on a latte leaned over and said, "You better put that up," pointing to the hundred-dollar bill bookmarker. Looking at the man, I smiled and said, "Oh, it's only a book marker!"

Smiling back, he said, "Okay!"

I picked up the bookmarker I had been using for months and turned it over and over examining it further. To my astonishment, I realized that the bookmarker was indeed a real hundred-dollar bill, fresh off the mint!

Sometimes we seers need to be shaken to see what is right in front of us. When I returned home and told Lorrie, the look on her face said it all.

Right after that experience, I had a dream and was taken into the heavenly realm. There I was kneeling in front of the Throne with my head bowed down. I heard the Lord ask me, "What is your birth name?"

I considered for a moment if this was a trick question, and raising my head slightly, I answered, "Ramon."

I heard Him respond, "I gave you that name. Use it." I was immediately back in my bed, now wide-awake pondering what had just happened. From that moment on, I began using my birth name, instead of Ray. Researching my name, I found out the Spanish meaning of my name is "mighty protector" and/or "defender of the people." My thoughts immediately went to my MorningStar divine appointments, the words spoken over me there,[28] and the fact that I have been interceding since my youth for people.[29] I realized then that I have been living up to my birth name without even knowing it. Names have a lot of meaning and great influence in a person's life.

In early August 2004, the Lord said me, "Go see Randy Clark at the conference in October." I told Lorrie and she purchased tickets for the conference that would be held at our church, but I was still reluctant to go. Through visions and dreams, I had been

---

28 See chapter 8.
29 See chapter 4.

given a revelation about TV gospel celebrities in the eighties and nineties who would fall from grace. I told Lorrie what I saw, and we read about it coming to pass in the newspaper a few years later. After watching these popular preachers fall, I was leery of opening up to any, even those who were sincere. I have since learned we all make mistakes, and our eyes need to be kept on Jesus Christ rather than men,

ANOINTED FIRES

The conference started and Lorrie attended, but I did not. Towards the end of the conference, I was at home one day, kicking back in the recliner watching TV when suddenly I heard the loud and audible Voice, "I told you to go see Randy Clark."

Immediately, I fired up my Harley and headed for the conference. Just as I walked in the door of the conference, I got such a jolt from the Holy Spirit. I walked with Lorrie to review the resources on the book tables in the lobby. While she was purchasing a book, I walked over to another table with more resources and got a nudge in the Spirit. Unsure what the Spirit was saying I reached for a book and nothing happened. As I reached for another book, I was nudged again by the Spirit. I picked up the book *Lighting Fires* by Randy Clark and handed it to Lorrie to purchase. The rest of this conference consisted of impartations and unseen encounters which I will cover later in this book.

I had finished reading the book *Lighting Fires* and now needed something to read while on an airplane ride to another conference in Colorado, "*The Advanced Wild at Heart Boot Camp.*" Scanning the bookshelf at my home office for a something to read, the Holy Spirit nudged me as I came upon *The Anointing* by Benny Hinn. As I reached out again, I felt a second nudge by the Spirit that jerked my head to the side. Grabbing the book off the shelf, I headed out the door to the airport.

I started reading the book in the terminal as I waited for boarding. This book stimulated a craving in my heart the more

I read it. While reading this book, I looked up and saw warriors all about me from the past, present, and future. I saw their way of life and the knowledge and wisdom they carried that comes from battles. I understood that the warriors carried that which came from the Lord. I watched them receive their counsel as I tried to take hold of it.

While absorbing *The Anointing*, I was praying one of the prayers Benny Hinn penned in the book. Over and over and over again during the flight, as the cravings grew, I prayed, *I will pay the price no matter the cost...I will pay the price, Lord, no matter the cost.* I had to know for myself if the things that I heard and read about from others in ministry, as well as in this book, were really true. Hearing stories of people being thrown across the room as the power of God was being released through them reminded me that I had been thrown and tossed as a child by unseen forces.[30]

The plane landed and I went to Hertz Car Rental for an SUV that I had reserved and to meet up with Wes, a fellow member of the band of brothers. Wes and I were sharing the cost of the two-hour drive into the Colorado mountains where the conference was being held. We talked on and off along the drive to the retreat. During the quiet times, my thoughts focused on the book I had read on the plane. My heart continued to echo its hunger as I prayed under my breath over and over between the lulls in our conversation,

I need to know, Lord. I need to know...I will pay the price no matter the cost...

When we arrived at our destination, I let Wes out at the front door to go into the registration lodge. Backing up the vehicle, I prayed one last time that same prayer as I parked, *Lord, I will pay the price, and I put my trust in Your hands, Father. Amen.*

I got out of the SUV and walked into the lodge and headed to the registration podium. Reaching out my hand to take the

---

30 See chapter 4.

form, I suddenly got hit across the left side of my jaw and was spun around 180 degrees from the impact of the strike. It felt like a right hook in a boxing match but much more powerful than I had ever felt. I blacked out for what I think was a fraction of a second and woke just as my face was about to hit the floor. I caught myself with one or both hands —I don't recall—before hitting the ground in a push-up position just as my nose was about to touch the floor. I reached up and grabbed the podium top as I started to pull myself up. Getting one knee under me and raising my head, I got hit again with what felt like an overhand punch in boxing. This time as the blow connected, the one knee that was under me kept me from hitting the floor as it didn't knock me out this time. There was this extreme throbbing in my jaw yet there was no pain. There was an aching, but yet it didn't hurt. There was no way to explain the type of soreness and tenderness that followed.

As I tried to stand, I was instantly overwhelmed with joy, peace, and love. I began to fill out the registration form for check-in. The staff behind the registration counter, and others in the room, were just staring at me in astonishment and uncertainty, looking for an understanding of the moment. When I had finished checking in, I went directly to my room with no cares, just feeling happy and full of joy. Arriving at my room, all I could do was put my stuff down on the floor in front of the bunk and lay my head on the bed to rest and just be in the presence of God, as this manifestation of His presence was a first-time experience for me. I felt, in a way, like a cartoon character seeing angels while stumbling around.

The Wild at Heart Advance began about 7:00 PM, and I was still in the joy of that Holy Spirit encounter all through the evening. I had no idea what was happening around me. The next thing I knew, it was early morning with the sun arising soon. I went to my room as most of the others were in their bunks asleep or just waking up. I fell into a deep sleep from the encounter and became the alarm clock for a few of my bunkmates with a rhythmic trumpeting snore.

How does one analyze being struck by an unseen force resulting in a greater ability to see in different realms of time? This was a new beginning for me, and I knew it was a result of that hunger and prayer from my heart: *I will pay the price no matter the cost, I put my trust in you, Lord.*

Finishing the book *The Anointing* I went out to join the others. I was learning to open myself up to trusting others more even when it seems they are less capable of doing what is needed to be done, especially while relying on them to do their part on a 40-foot high ropes course! Ever been at the "dead man drop" with a 90-pound girl being your only leverage from killing yourself? It is during exercises like these that you can see how much more growth you need, particularly when there has been a personal blind spot.

This is not as hard to conceive when you think about technological advances. We know our paycheck will be in the bank on payday even though we did nothing specific to get it there. In the same way, God does the greater things on our behalf every day, and all we have to do is say, "Thank You." Putting your trust in His hands when the Actual presence manifests is a part of exercising a giant leap of faith.

The retreat continued to flow, and I heard these words throughout the conference, "It is time to go to Toronto."

The final morning at Advance, while watching the sun come over the edge of a mountain top and penetrate into the valley as the light displaced the darkness of night below, all of us standing there could hear God speaking to us so clearly. In that awesome moment, I saw prayers being answered from the heavens by angels descending into homes through roof tops. Looking now over those at the Advance, I saw officers of the heavenly hosts being released as new orders came from beams of light and other angelic hosts.

Driving back to the airport I heard the directive again: *Go to the conference in Toronto.*

We reached the airport, turned in the rental car, and saying good-bye, Wes and I parted ways. I called Lorrie from the terminal phone and told her I was going to Toronto, Canada.

"Do you want to come?" I asked her.

"Well, I have been trying to get you to go there for the past five years," she said.

"No, you haven't." I said. "This is the first time I have heard of the place. I am going to Toronto in January. Do you want to go?"

"YES! YES! YES!" Lorrie replied excitedly. That's it. I knew we were going to Toronto, but where and to what conference was still to be revealed.

I started checking the internet for Toronto events that next month, and Toronto Airport Christian Fellowship (TACF)[31] was the place that was revealed. The Holy Spirit nudged me again on the Pastors and Leaders Conference at the end of January 2005. It also included a "soaking school" two days before the conference started. I felt compelled and curious to attend, so I registered us and purchased our tickets to Toronto.

This new step in my prayer being answered opened me up to whole new revelations of the Holy Spirit in expecting more.

I will pay the price no matter the cost. I put my trust in you, Lord. This epiphany brought a new bonding relationship with the Holy Spirit as my Friend, Coach, Trainer, Partner, Companion, and Lord. Bodily manifestations were now a natural occurrence reflecting things I asked, confirmed, released, or declared. My body would begin to manifest itself as I would ask questions and receive answers and as I would give words of knowledge through sight, sound, visions, and other means. It was like the Holy Spirit would smack me on the back or part of my body causing me to jerk upward or forward, just like when you smack a friend when you say a hardy hello. I loved knowing the Lord was with me always.

31

To some, these manifestations were a little distracting, but to me, I knew I was doing the right thing.

As it turned out, our trip to Toronto corresponded with the ten-year anniversary celebration of the Holy Spirit outpouring there which started in 1994. Since that time, thousands of people had come from around the world to experience the love of the Father with manifestations of healing from His presence. Many who came carried back the Fire of Love with them to their cities and countries as the Holy Spirit's presence released more of the Father's love with greater manifestations of healings, restorations, signs and wonders.

I knew for sure I was doing what I was supposed to do, as favor followed us. I had reserved a small compact car from Hertz rental. When I got to the rental counter at the airport, the agent told me, "Sorry we have no economy, compact, midsize, or full size cars available at this time." We were actually upgraded to a Jaguar with GPS navigation for the full week, and they threw in an extra day at no charge. We were so shocked at the upgrade, thanking the clerk and God. Then as we looked around the Hertz lot while heading for the Jaguar in its space, we observed plenty of cars in the spaces ready to be rented. Again, we gave a big "Thank You!" to God as we took our upgraded Jaguar.

We arrived at the Marriott Hotel, checked-in, and were upgraded to the business suite! Very nice! Diagonally across the street from the hotel, we noticed a coffee shop called "2nd Cup." This was not just a natural upgrade but supernatural as things like this continued through the whole week we were in Toronto.

On the way to the TACF facility, and just a few blocks before arriving at the church, the atmosphere shifted and we could feel angelic presence. The closer we got to the facility, the heavier the presence got. As we walked into the front door of the building, we noticed a misty-type of cloud in the air. People were laid out all over the building before the evening service began. We explored the huge building which held a cafeteria, bookstore, upstairs conference rooms, and a children's area with carved wooden animals hung on the wall all around its doorway.

There was also a large room behind the stage reserved for prayer and soaking where music was being played continually. Looking inside the room from the doorway, we saw the room had beautiful prophetic art, Scriptures, flags, and dancing in the center of the room. We went back into the sanctuary just to sit down for a while to absorb the presence.

Having left our home in the very early morning hours, we were exhausted from the flight and hungry, so we returned to the hotel. On the way back, we decided to stop at the 2nd Cup coffee shop to get a snack. My thoughts went to a lyric from the song "Dive" by Steven Curtis Chapman, "Standing on the edge over the river there is only one direction for me and there is no turning back. I'll take a leap of faith; the river is wide, the water is deep, sink or swim, I'm diving in."

I said to the Lord, *I am diving in; this water I am in is uncharted waters; I am going for a swim after You.* At the same time Lorrie heard the Dionne Warwick song in 2nd Cup, "Do you know the way to San Jose?" That song soon came into play on the journey in San Jose.

Chapter Ten

TORONTO, ENGLAND & PARIS

THE NIGHT WENT QUICKLY with anticipation of the first day of class. We had no idea what "soaking" was. The group meetings were in The Ark, and there we learned that soaking was another form of prayer. This form has always been around known as conative[32] prayer starting in the Scriptures with Enoch. That afternoon, June Bain, the leader came over to me as I was standing in the back of the class. This woman Lorrie describes as having the purest water she has ever seen.

During soaking time, I received a word of knowledge from the Lord for Suzie, a priest's wife, and it had such a heaviness resonating on and in me. I started crying as tears were running down my face and I crumbled under the weight after releasing the word to this woman. I spun around to lean on a chair after delivery, and I screamed out in agony as I had never felt before. The others continued releasing words of knowledge to Suzie. This occurrence had a profound effect on me as well as the intended recipient.

"Flushed" is the best way I could describe what was happening to me as issues that resided in me had to go so I could continue to handle what was being released through me. This told me we don't always have to be in perfect order to do His will. He has everything in control in restoration of two people at the same time. The rest of the day moved swiftly past as I was being reformatted to handle

---

32 Oxford Dictionaries: *Grammar* denoting a word or structure that expresses attempted action as opposed to action itself.

a greater capacity for what was to come, all the while having very little awareness of anything happening.

The next morning was a crisp and beautiful winter morning with a couple of feet of snow on the ground even though the sun was shining brightly. Inside the building, you could feel the heat of the sun passing through the glass windows of The Ark. It was during that morning session I suddenly remembered that a team from VVCLC in California was heading out on a mission trip to India. I excused myself and went into an attached room in The Ark used for storage. I called Dave who was heading on the trip, wished them well, and blessed them. After hanging up I proceeded to pray and intercede for them.

I started with the basic prayers of open doors, good travel, and protection. Then as I was saying the word "protection," it began to overwhelm me as though I was going to burst. My prayers changed as I remembered all the unnatural things that happened to me as a child. I started praying aloud for the release of legions of angels for protecting those going on the trip. Instantly I saw a commander warrior angel looking up to the heavens for approval then quickly disappear. I continued praying as if in a military campaign as I released more angels as our Father allowed it.

I then realized in my thoughts that fallen angels are demons and they are under Christ Jesus' submission as are all angels. My prayers changed to calling forth the hidden angels to join the assigned angels for the team and mission in order to bring breakthrough. I called in an angelic covering from the four degrees north, south, east, and west of that nation. I started moving angelic flanks into different positions in the various regions of India. I commanded angels of various kinds from supply, healing, warrior, and regional angels to the places the team was going, commanding that they were to hold the territory that is taken in the name of the Lord Jesus. Then just as I was starting to give more commands, I heard a very loud the audible Voice: "*I will pick your battles.*"

I looked around, then looked up to the heavens with fear and trembling as I fell to my knees saying, "I'm sorry, I'm sorry, I'm sorry. Please, please forgive me," and that ended the prayer.

I went back into the other room where everyone was soaking in the presence of the Lord and buried my face in the carpet in a prone position. A few minutes later a TACF soaking team member came over to me as I was trembling and still apologizing in fear. Nakamura came over to me, laid hands on me and said, "The Lord told me to tell you, 'He will pick your battles.'"

Then a peace came over me as Nakamura was laying hands on me, and I spent the rest of the day laying in the Lord's presence. Unable to move, I laid there as others from the team came and prayed for me. Then I felt a rearranging going on inside of me.

I have believed since my youth that a few individuals have the authority to move angels. If you, as a man, can judge angels[33] and Jesus acknowledges you before the angels[34], then you can release them in the authority and power given to you in the releasing of God will. The Holy Spirit released these verses to me when I was seeking answers in the middle of a discussion one day with a fellow Christian leader who disagreed.

Having laid there motionless for a time, I began to see balls of fire hitting me as well as going through me from head to toe, and I was being consumed by the fire. My palms were getting hit by the balls of fire, and I started to jolt and twitch with each hit as the fire was replaced by lightning or great volts of electricity

---

33 1 Corinthians 6:3.
34 Luke 12:8, Revelation 3:5.

which was flowing from one palm to another with precision and intensity. All I could do was sit up and watch. As I tried to throw a ball of flame that was in my hand I heard, "*I will teach you how to throw it.*"

There was another in the group who could see the balls of fire, and we began playing catch with them. More people in the group began to see the flaming balls and some others joined in. We threw the ball and hit some of the group. They went down and out under the Spirit for quite a while.

It was graduation night with a special dinner in the upstairs rooms for those who attended the soaking school. The presence was so intense that a few others and I left the dinner table and went to sit on the floor outside the banquet room. We were afraid of collapsing into our food on the table. We arose in time to receive our diplomas from John and Carol Arnott, the senior leaders. This was the first of many trips for me to TACF as I was evolving in the natural and supernatural.

In September 2005, Lorrie and I decided to start a soaking secession each Tuesday night in the prayer room at our church, The Mission (formerly called VVCLC), and it continues to this day. This has also led to other soaking secessions and schools in Northern California. We learned to rest in the Lord's presence while finding peace from life's circumstances, and it only takes a little time each day.

Soaking involves getting away from everyone—shutting a door, going for a walk—with a simple prayer not asking for anything but experiencing His wisdom, peace, knowledge, and understanding. With no agendas, soaking is putting on some worship music to rest and just wait on the Lord as He comes.

I have learned to keep a pencil and some paper handy (or a recording device) to record what is received from the Lord while in the soaking state.

The Louvre Entrance, Paris, with Wayne, Diane, and Lorrie

ENGLAND AND PARIS

In the spring of 2005, Lorrie and I joined a team lead by Dan McCollam to Bradford, England, to visit Ronnie Moore, a colleague of Dan's. Ronnie was preaching out of one of the same buildings that Smith Wigglesworth the evangelist of the 19th century had used. Wigglesworth was known for his healing ministry and his ability to raise the dead as Jesus and Holy Spirit moved through him. Many of Wigglesworth's miracles have been documented in medical journals.

It was here in this building that I sought the gift of tongues. I had never wanted any part of tongues since I didn't understand what was being said. I repented for what I had said about the gift. Dan prayed for me, and it was released to me. I was like a baby who first learns to talk, and as I continued, more and more of the language began to flow. This new gift empowered all my abilities. It reminded me of the fictional character Popeye the Sailorman when he ate his spinach and gained supernatural strength to stop the bad guys.

There in England, my intercessory role took on another level relative to the extra strength that was needed in the numinous realms. It was on Friday night while we were worshiping and dancing that I saw a pastor from Africa, who was also visiting the church, in a vision in a wheel chair. Saying nothing to him, I only interceded in prayer. This vision continued over three days, and then it was gone. I knew I had interceded to prevent this disastrous occurrence from happening, having confirmed it with Dan. This began to release in me a hunger for increase in interceding which brings a greater measure of responsibility that we can walk in.

The trip to England came to a close but Lorrie and I, along with Wayne and Diane LaCosse, had decided to visit Paris, France, just across the channel. Checking into a bed and breakfast, we quickly went off to see the sights. I continually pursued the issue of going downtown to the Harley Davidson store to get a Harley Davidson (HD) polo shirt that had "Paris Harley Davidson" embroidered on it.

Protestors

Crossing the river, we found the streets lined with locals by the tens of thousands protesting about jobs and work status. There were police riot squads located at every corner and along the side streets off the main strip. I walked the opposite direction of the protesters to reach the HD store, hoping they might still be open even though the majority of the stores were closed because of the protestors.

During the stroll down the side streets, I got visions of autos and vans with bombs in them. I asked the group to pray as we walked. We prayed that the hidden things would be revealed and found, that no one would get hurt, and those responsible would be apprehended.

During the walk, I saw three diverse visions each in a different location along the few miles we walked to get to the HD store. I was so determined to get that HD shirt, hoping for favor, but the store was closed when we arrived. We turned around and headed back to visit the Notre Dame Cathedral, continuing in intercession until the weight of praying was gone. Notre Dame was worth the walk.

The next morning the French Newspaper showed a van and other vehicles that had been seized with bombs in them. We recognized in the photos the vicinity where we had walked and interceded the day previous.

This event, along with other occurrences in Europe, had me pressing into the prayer language of tongues even though I did not know fully what it meant. It soon became like getting a second wind of energy, being refreshed to endure to the end. The trip came to an end, and we returned to California. These unseen occurrences of intercession are needed to prevent incidences in the natural.

A ro'eh (seer) changes circumstances. When you see something in the Spirit, it becomes your responsibility to intercede, as doing so can change the outcome. Those who get prophetic revelations are like time travelers. You transverse space, time, and matter for making this a better world as God gives you insight for the sake of His children.

Notre Dome

This trip opened our hearts to taking a missions trip to see what God was doing instead of a vacation. We prepared for this by taking a missions training class run by Bill and Carol Dew.[35] It was in this class we learned about *sozo*, a Greek word meaning "complete healing," "deliverance," and "restoration."

During the training, I made a 2 "x 3.5" bi-fold cheat-sheet card to carry with me with notes on the sozo details that I did not want to mess up on. It became very useful in heated spiritual confrontations when my natural mind would go blank on the front line.

It is good to remember that the empowering of just one of the spiritual gifts enhances the other abilities as well. I have found

---

35 www.dewnamis.com

that to be true with speaking in tongues; it is a higher gift.[36] It is not a question of whether this ability comes from God. The question becomes, "How much will the Holy Spirit release of it?" We each have a calling set before us. As we take the journey, we have opportunity to use our abilities or to not use them. We can and do, at times, work together as one with God in making this a better world.

The baptism of the Holy Spirit is needed today more than ever. When ministering in sozo, praying for the person to be freshly filled with the Holy Spirit will make all the difference in the world if they are willing and wanting to know Jesus Christ. The Holy Spirit comes into their life, fills them anew, and brings healing with restoration."

UNDERSTANDING

Bob Jones, one of the great-grandfathers of the prophetic, introduced this concept of understanding of the natural gifts. Let's say you are standing in a room. Down the hall there is hot bread baking in the kitchen oven. As the aroma fills the building, what do you smell? (Answer: bread.)

If you walk into the kitchen and your sinuses are plugged up so you cannot smell what would you see? (Answer: bread.)

If you are wearing a blindfold outside the building and someone from inside the building brings a piece of the bread and puts it in your mouths, what would you taste? (Answer: Bread.)

Another blindfolded person has a piece of bread put into his hands. What does he feel? (Answer: bread.)

Each of these senses tells you the answer is bread.

Knowing something is being released when there are no clues is your senses coming alive telling you otherwise. (Could it be prophetic? Yes.) You cannot hear bread, but you know it is bread because of your other senses. That is the same way prophetic senses

---

36 1Corinthians 12:31

work as Holy Spirit speaks to you for interceding. In my book *Seers in the Kingdom: (Their Stories)*, I tell of journeys in which hearing was hard and sight was being obscured but the smell of sulfur and the taste of other elements told of what was afoot in the unseen realm.

Chapter Eleven

THE AWAKENING

HAVING FINISHED THE MISSION training under the Dews and Boxes, it is now August 2005. Lorrie and I are joining Randy Clark, a global evangelist, on his team for a two-week mission trip. Scheduled to minister in Brazil in the cities of San Paulo, Fiero De Santana, Belo Horizonte, and Belem, we were looking to walk in the grace of empowerment on our first short-term mission trip. The teams consisted of working people from different countries who were using their vacation time to make a difference in the world. This team consisted of 48 people, each member seeking a greater understanding of the Gospel in signs and wonders and greatly desiring to be a part of it.

The first meeting was held at a hall in Fiero De Santa which had a seating capacity of 4,000. The second team would arrive the following two weeks to continue the crusade, and we would overlap for three days for the Coliseum Healing Crusade in the city of Belem with a 14,000 capacity. The Nazarene Churches of Brazil were our hosts; they expected an overflow of people for healings at the Coliseum. In preparation, Randy sent Bill and Carol Dew as apostles a month ahead to train up the leaders and teams from local churches in Brazil that would be needed.

The first day began with a mission briefing at the hotel followed by impartations and prayer. When it came time to depart for the first meeting, two of the team members, Brian from The Mission and Eric from Alaska, had to be carried onto the bus because of the anointing released during the impartations. This verse immediately came to mind and was felt.

> *But you shall receive power (ability, efficiency, and might) when the Holy Spirit has come upon you, and you shall be My witnesses in Jerusalem and all Judea and Samaria and to the ends (the very bounds) of the earth.* Acts 1:8

Now being ambassadors for the Kingdom with power and authority, the team arrived at the conference a few hours early to pray, prepare, and get acclimated to the new atmosphere, or should I say water. "This water was different in Brazil," I thought as I considered what my friend Eugene Ray said.

> *It is like taking some fish out of their aquarium and putting them into a river with other creatures of the river. What was a normal thing for the fish of the river was a new experience to those from the aquarium. The river fish had become accustom to the threats, paying them no mind until the last possible moment and, at times, until it was too late. The new fish saw the threats right away, having just come out of the aquarium habitat. If you took the river fish and put them in the aquarium, it would be the same for them. The new fish saw what the native fish of the river did not see and could take action.*

There was an intercessor group led by Tracee Loosle which Lorrie joined. I volunteered for the deliverance squad to do sozo. I had spent months taking a class along with reading books and manuals like *Listen to me Satan* by Carlos Annacondia, *Wrestling with Dark Angels* by Dr. C. Peter Wagner, *How to cast out Demons* by Doris Wagner, and *Spiritual Warfare* by (Bridge) Michael Harper, to name a few. I was a rookie with nothing but the book know-how. Boy and was I ever getting a new awakening!

I went into the conference hall to help with the setup. A few others walked the grounds and saturated the area in prayer. I observed local leaders of the community setting up areas for private prayer behind curtains. When I asked why the private chambers, they stated, "If something happens in the event, it will not disrupt the conference. You will understand once the conference begins." Those areas, I realized, were for sozo healings.

Walking around the conference hall a bit bored, waiting for the conference to start, I was looking out the windows and doors at all the surroundings. A young man followed behind me, keeping his distance, and I kept an eye on him in my peripheral vision. Then, suddenly and out of nowhere, three of the other team members along with a local pastor grabbed the young man and dragged him behind one of the curtained areas. I turned and asked another team member what was going on. He responded, "Didn't you see his face and eyes?"

"No," I answered.

"The young man's eyes where all white and rolled up in his head," he told me, "and he was following you around. He is possessed, having an unclean spirit."

I went behind the curtain where they had taken the young man. There was one man at each arm with one behind him as he sat with the inquisitor in front of him. His eyes were pure white with no pupil. He was turning his head, observing everything around him, but saying nothing.

I was told a local pastor sent someone to find his mother who was also attending the conference. The man returned quickly bringing the mother. He asked her to have a seat, pointing to a chair behind him. The inquisitor paused for a moment, got up and walked over to me. Pulling me aside, he gave me a list of questions that he needed the mother to answer. The young man could not speak, or would not speak, because of the unclean spirit.

I took the mother into another area since she did speak English and asked her the questions given me. When I had finished with those, I received more questions from the Holy Spirit to ask her. I delivered all these answers back to the inquisitor to help with the extrication of the young man.

The mother told us about a pact her son made with a female red witch. He had given money to her at the age of 14 in order to be a great football player. She gave him a liquid potion which he drank. She gave him a bracelet that he was told he must always wear to be a great football player.

The question from the Holy Spirit I was given for him was, "Did you have a relationship with the red witch?"

"No," he answered.

"Did you sleep with her?" I asked.

"Yes," he replied, "many times."

The leader of the group, having this information, exorcised the unclean spirit. The young man was restored back to normal and his eyes and other facial features returned to normal. This, being my first sozo, left me with a new understanding of what still exists around the world today. This was the first step toward more healing that needed to be done. The unclean spirit could return with seven more stronger unclean spirits if the empty space had not been filled with Holy Spirit. The root to the demonic possession was found through the questions. The young man had removed and destroyed artifacts that connected him to the witch and root. The young man continued seeking me throughout the conference for prayer. I used that time to continue to see him filled him with the Holy Spirit as I was led by Holy Spirit and then referred him back to his pastor.

THE GLORY RAIN

Later that night at the conference, Randy asked the worship leader if he could play the song "*Let it Rain*" by Michael W. Smith. It was during this song that the atmosphere changed, becoming very concentrated with a misty cloud that I actually saw. As the worship continued, I started seeing colored rain drops the size of silver dollars falling on the people. Then suddenly people started yelling and cheering in both English and Portuguese which is

Brazil's native language. The team was wondering what was going on as they looked all around.

Then one of the local pastors ran up on the stage carrying a boy of about 4 to 5 years of age. The crowd was going ballistic when they saw the little boy standing next to him. What was revealed to us, the team and other strangers to the area, was that this little boy had never walked a day in his life. During worship and praise he got up and started walking around. The pastor set him down, and the boy took two steps very slowly forward. It was like the cheering at a football stadium when a goal is made as his mother ran up with tears of joy saying, "Thank you, anomie *de Jesus.*"

This was the first of the signs and wonders which took place on this awakening trip through Brazil. This is the first fragment of testimonies to be unbridled. These mysterious miracles would open our hearts and minds, bringing the signs and wonders of the evolutionary time we are in from city to city.

Randy with the boy who had never walked

THE POWER OF FORGIVENESS

The team ministered at a local Nazarene Church. A beautiful, sandy blonde woman with her friend was sitting in the back of the church crying. The friend of the woman came up to me asking for prayer for her friend, telling us that her friend could not open her hands and was in pain. The mission team's rule was women prayed for women and men prayed for men. The only exception was for the leaders. There was no one available as every team member was tied up praying for someone. I went to the team leader and asked what to do. The leader said to me, "The Lord is using you. Go pray for her now." I knew then this was meant for me to do.

I went over to the woman. Seeing her hands and fingers were locked in a ridged form much like a person with severe arthritis and seeing that there was no swelling, I inquired of the Lord about what was causing this ailment in her hands. I heard Him say, "Ask her when it started and what she was doing?"

She answered, "It began almost a week ago. I had just broken up with my boyfriend who was having an affair. It started that night." With tears running down her cheeks, I laid hands on her shoulder, and she fell to the floor in the fetal position under the power of the Holy Spirit. I began speaking to her that healing would come through forgiveness. I knew she had to forgive the ex-boyfriend as hate is the root to many illnesses.

"Forgiving him," I instructed her, "will set you free. He is not here in pain; you are. Forgiveness is what is needed in your heart." We began speaking aloud of forgiveness in prayer to Jesus. By the end of the night, when it was time to go, one hand was back to normal and able to move all around, and the other hand was almost normal. We thanked the Lord, asking the Holy Spirit to come fill her.

This is a great example of what hate can do and how forgiveness can heal and restore. Remember you don't have to like a person to forgive them. You have to forgive them in your heart as the

Lord knows your heart. It doesn't mean you have to seek them out, although in some cases that is necessary.

The next day I went to a pre-meeting for the leaders' retreat happening that night, and Randy asked me to be his armor bearer. I wasn't sure what to do or what it meant, but I accepted the position knowing it was of great importance. It was after accepting I felt this weighty-like robe or mantel come upon my shoulders and head, and it became as light as a feather. I held this position for about a week and then felt it was time to ask to be released from being Randy's armor bearer. Knowing the Lord was now moving me into a new position, I was released by Randy and a new armor bearer took my place: "He is in good hands."

In the final days of this trip in Brazil with both ministry teams there for the three-day Coliseum Crusade, I kept hearing, "Go to intercession," at different times throughout the day and night.

I tried to ignore this instruction because of a poor experience with intercessors in my past. I was a fighter, and of all the intercessors I had ever known, none of them had any kind of stomach for a good fight. I was looking for a good fight—to be a conqueror—in this journey. That is why I joined the sozo group on the team. In this position, you saw the enemy and kicked his butt by setting people free. As I sat with the sozo team, I heard the Voice again, though not gentle as before, "*Go to intercession.*" I responded, "I'll go later."

As the crusade at the coliseum progressed that night, I heard those words again with a stern urgency, "Go to intercession!"

Again I replied, "I'll go later, after deliverance." I did not want to go, but curiosity was weighing in now because of the persistence of the Voice. It was hard to leave the excitement going on with the deliverance teams. In the bleachers, going through the crowds, were teams bringing people manifesting demons to the sozo teams which were positioned in the back of the stadium so as not to disrupt the conference. This was my warrior's dream of smiting the enemy.

The people who were manifesting unclean spirits were immediately carried to the back of coliseum to the sozo teams. This particular night was worse than the first night in *Fiero De Santa*. I saw individuals spitting stuff out of their mouth at the sozo teams that smelled of death and sulfur and had colors from yellowish to greenish. This brought a recollection of how Clarrisa Watkins and others with her held a woman down on the floor at the first conference in Brazil. The woman smelled of sulfur and manifests this green stuff out of her mouth as the demonic spirit convulsed and cursed at everyone until a female leader came over and, with love, set her free.

INTERCESSION

Back to event at hand. There were others manifesting who were climbing the walls like spiders and hanging on the walls. There was one person throwing team members around without even touching them, until finally another team leader commanded the demon to stop and be still in the name of Jesus, rendering the person motionless. I sat through three deliverances that night and saw these people set free. At one point no more people were being brought under the lanai for deliverance.. I knew this was my queue to go to the intercession team, and looking up into the heavens I said, "Okay Lord, I'm going to intercession." Excusing myself and asking to be released, I went into the building that held the intercessory team. Not surprisingly, as soon as I walked in the building door, the sozo areas began to overflow again with people who had unclean spirits.

I was pondering on what was next with the Lord when my mind went blank as I entered the building that held the intercessors. This building was over 400 years old and had a jail cell ten feet from the front door. There was a little corridor to the right and a set of spiral stairs. The cell door was open, and the intercessory team was in the cell doing intercession. I immediately felt very uncomfortable, losing all transition of thought and feeling filthy all over as I walked through the cell door. Turning to leave the cell room and sit down instead on the stairs, I said, "I'm here Lord." Then Tracee, the head intercessor, came over to me. I felt there was an angelic presence with her. She asked why I didn't come into the cell, and I responded, "I feel filthy, dirty, and unclean."

Tracee paused as if listening before replying and said, "Let's get you cleaned off" and brushed off my shoulders and back with the wave of her hand. Instantly I felt clean again and stood up to join the team. Tracee stated, "When people are being set free from unclean spirits, those spirits are on the hunt to find a new home." That made perfect sense.[37] I always ask the Holy Spirit now to fill the empty places in all things.

Then Tracee proceeded to give instructions to me, "Before you say anything about what you see in the spirit realm, please tell me first, and I will decide the time to release the information to the others." I listened for a while to what was happening in the intercession team. I whispered in a quiet prayer, "This was not like any intercession I have been in Lord. I'll try it, but if there is any problem with the people, I won't do it again."

Immediately I began to see things. Walking over to Tracee, I began to speak quietly into her ear about the things that I saw in the mystical realm. The first image was a giant sword that came down from the sky and struck itself into the ground. At that, she looked at me, pointing to the others with her finger, she said and to a certain person, "Speak what you saw. Three different people had the same confirmation."

I also saw daggers and mini swords flying through the air just before the sword struck the ground. These were the lies of the enemy, and there were more forces coming to try and hold the

---

37 Luke 11:24.

ground. The sword was from the Lord coming to take back His processions and land that had been stolen. I see it this way:

> *Simply, the Sword is the Holy Spirit working through us and with us in the affairs of God. The shield of faith protects us from the daggers, darts, and mini swords that come trying to create turmoil. Putting on the armor of God is necessary for all of us. The transforming of our minds is a very big part of this as we put on the helmet of salvation. I see it protects and it also allows our minds to comprehend the depth of what is needed to go beyond the normal. It is when we take territory in the natural that it is also taken in the spiritual/mystical dimensions.[38]*
>
> *The binding and releasing on earth are keys that hold fast to the other realms.[39] That is why when territory is taken in the natural, Christians must occupy the territory, or more force comes in to take control.[40]*

This ended the first night of intercession at the coliseum. Many other things began to unfold as the conference continued. The next evening at the crusade without being told and before the coliseum doors were even opened, with the intercessors and the sozo teams were already at work. The grounds at the rear of the building had a garden with a fountain statue where the pre-service intercession was taking place. There was a lot of heavenly warfare as I and other seers observed what was going on in the garden area as the sozo team was setting people free. Standing in the middle of the garden area was an angelic host about three stories tall with a shield and sword while other angelic and unclean spirits were fighting in the unseen realms. Many of the unclean spirits cast out where trying to find new homes. We watched as people unknowingly touched the

---

38 Ephesians 6.
39 Matthew 16:19, 18:17
40 Luke 11:26

outlining sphere of the angelic being's leg and or foot and then would collapse from the immanence of the angel.

The building was finally opened to allow the intercessor team in, but the cell door was locked and the foyer was too small for the group. We explored other parts of the building by climbing up the spiral stairs to the second floor. This second level had a heavy presence of unclean spirits. Even as I walked up the spiral stairs, I could feel the same type of presence, though much stronger, just like when I was thrown off of my bicycle as a child.[41] There was nothing visible except a small statue of the Virgin Mary on a protruding wall shelf. I was trying to shake off the feeling, and it left when I reached the second floor.

The second stepping stone: releasing.

We found out from the grounds keeper that the building had once been a doctor office and that this doctor had murdered his patients in order to gain power in black and red magic back in the 14th or 15th century. This doctor kept patients in the cell and used the rooms on the second floor for the rituals. The group went back outside under the lanai, and Tracee asked a few team members to spiritually clean the place up by removing the unclean residue that still lingered in the mystic realm.

While under the lanai during intercession, I saw a vision of a left hand, demonic in appearance, reaching into the lanai and stealing things. There was a right hand also, half human-half demonized, also appearing and disappearing. The intercessor team, being right next to the sozo team, was having huge warfare in the mystic realm. Tracee sent David, Brian, and another lady to do more spiritual cleaning in the upstairs of the building so we could move the intercessory team there.

The third stepping stone: asking and walking in His might.

I received permission to go with them. As we were climbing up the spiral stairs, I felt that same strange feeling again looking

---

41 See chapter 3.

around, all I could see was the statue of the Virgin Mary. Once again, the feeling was gone once we passed by it on the way upstairs. Then while returning to the group downstairs, the feeling relapsed. When I got back under the lanai, the vision recurred again. I asked the Lord what to do, and His response was: *Stomp on it.*

When the demonic hand reappeared to steal, I stomped on it in the mystic realm and in the natural. The next moment, as I was pondering what had happened from my stomp, the crew came out of the door and announced that the head of the Virgin Mary statue had just broken off as we were coming down the stairs. I then heard: *Throw it away, but do not touch it. This statue had been used and cursed in satanic rituals.*

Looking around and finding two rags and a garbage can lid, we went up the stairs, picked up the pieces of the statue, and threw them in the garbage outside. I received another vision: the right hand that was human but the thumb and two fingers were outlined with demonic darkness was back, and it was stealing things again. I told Tracee about the hand, but before I could finish the sentence, she said we have to get out of this area. Brian came up and said, "What you saw was unclean spirits trying to find a home on three people."

The men in the group grabbed the plastic stacking chairs from under the lanai as we headed for the stadium field where the crusade was going on. The team had to step over people blocking the path to the stadium in sozo. There on the ground, the last obstacle was a woman who had been a witch but was now set free. I was the last one to step over her, carrying some chairs. Suddenly, I got hit across my back and the force hurled me three to four feet forward.

Turning to see who hit me from behind and letting go of the chairs I was carrying, I saw that no one was there. Standing to the side, however, were a man and woman holding hands and watching the deliverance of the woman. They looked at me then turned and focused their attention in another direction. I picked the chairs back up and followed everyone out to the stadium field.

Just before reaching the stadium, I told Tracee what had just happened. She said, "Let's clean you off, and let the sozo team handle it," as I was looking to go back. I wanted to go back for a fight, and then realized how one might fight a mystical fight in a natural realm. This was a whole different type of fighting. I still had a lot to learn about using the armor of God.

Brian, another seer, spoke about the human hand with the outlined demonized two fingers and a thumb as we set up a circle of chairs in the field and sealed the circle with prayer. Brain said, "What you saw with the right hand was demons jumping back and forth between three people. They will try to get into the circle of intercession but will be unable as three people from the group stayed outside of the circle. Those unclean spirits were fishing trying to hook a catch." A short time later, because of the distractions going on, Tracee moved the intercessors back onto the bus for intercession.

Then I saw an angelic presence on the bus next to Tracee, myself, and some others. It was time to be excused from intercession. The Lord released me from staying with the intercessors. Tracee paused as I had seen another angel, after a moment of prayer and listening, she said to me, "You have been given a healing angel. Go and do as the Lord guides you, and I bless you." With new orders now and having the presence of two different angels assigned to me, I left the bus and went back onto crusade grounds. Lines were now forming by the hundreds on the spectator side of the fence.

This was a blast for me—being able to hit unclean spirits sending them flying out of the park in a whole new way, like a ball player hitting home runs, through partnering with the Holy Spirit and the Heavenly forces.

Chapter Twelve

THE STADIUM

I RETURNED BACK TO the stadium as Randy ministered in both English and Portuguese from the platform while the lines continued to increase. Checking in with Carol Dew, I told her what had transpired on the bus. She instructed me to join the healing teams forming out in the stadium field in preparation for those in lines for healing. It was later that evening, and the intercessors had come out to the stadium field to join the healing teams. These are a few of the stories of what Jesus did that night.

While observing some healing miracles done through the teams that I began to call natural or normal healings, I realized a funny thing. As you walk through these wonders and signs over two weeks, it becomes like reading—you come to expect them. It is important to remember the of giving thanks for allowing us to be able to participate in these healings, that we could do nothing without the Father, Son, and Holy Spirit, that Jesus is our Key to the keys that He gave us as princes and princesses[42] in showing His love for all His children.

In some cases, witchcraft was the cause of the ailment. The person was suffering from the presence of an unclean spirit brought through curses someone had spoken over them. There were times when the fight for healing was held in a stalemate that another upward stepping stone came into play for using the keys.[43] In one

---

[42] 1 Peter 2:9 But you are a chosen race, a royal priesthood, a holy nation, a people for his own possession, that you may proclaim the excellences of him who called you out of darkness into his marvelous light.

[43] Matthew 16:19 "I will give you the keys of the kingdom of heaven, and whatever you bind on earth shall be bound in heaven, and whatever you loose on earth shall be loosed in heaven."

instance, a woman was healed, but the symptom kept coming back before we could completely seal the healing. I kept hearing, "Look up." Standing about 30-feet away, I saw a person speaking something as she stared at the woman and then turned towards me. I knew then this was witchcraft in operation as the person stared me in the eyes as if to challenge me, but I was empowered by the Holy Spirit. I laid my hand on the woman being healed as a safeguard while observing that witch and rebuking her curses in Jesus' name. Turning my focus back again on the young woman in pain, I commanded healing into her body. She got up off the ground, jumping up and down with such joy and excitement at being completely healed. Thank you, Jesus.

Signs, miracles, and wonders take many forms to bring life to us and glory to God. The words of knowledge on the trip came at different levels, which I refer to as stepping stones, solid and firm. But in the numinous realms with the demonic forces at work, things can and will change. The Word is solid, but the application can break like a glass. The Word is always solid, but we must seek the Holy Spirit for the application. Nothing is impossible in any realm with the empowerment given to you in your gifts.

THREE TO ONE

Midnight was approaching fast with a few hundred who still needed healings. I was exhausted and found Lorrie to tell her I was done for the night. I went over in a corner of the field to lay down in the grass. She continued to pray for those in her line as the Lord healed them. In her line was an older man. The interpreter explained that the man's leg had been broken in three different places and had never completely healed.

Lorrie laid hands on him, praying for healing. When she had finished, the man turned to leave, still limping. Seeing he was not healed, Lorrie called him back. She stated, "You will not leave here unhealed," and the interpreter relayed that message, telling him to wait. Lorrie came over to me as I was resting on the ground, gave me a swift kick in the butt and said, "The Lord told me to get you. You are needed to pray for that man over there. His leg had been broken in three places and has not healed properly." That is a passion of the heart my wife has for others. There is no other like her to me. I wondered how lucky I was to be her husband.

Looking up, I took a deep breath and sighed, "Okay."

The man was leaning on his good leg with a look of disappointment on his face. I introduced myself and began by laying my hand on the man's head with a command for healing. Then everything went completely quiet—all the sound in the stadium was gone. The only thing I heard was the Voice, but quiet as never before: *Put your hands on his leg.*

Acting in response to the command, I put both of my hands on the man's leg, one on the inside and the other hand on the outside of his leg just below the knee cap where it had been broken. The Voice replied to my actions, "*Move your hands down his leg.*"

As I did move my hands down the leg, the break of the bone felt like the edge of a cliff under my hands and fingers. I stopped in bewilderment having never felt anything like this before. I continued moving my hands down the bone slowly so as not to miss anything, and then startled as I felt the bones shift. Pausing over the fracture, with the center of my palms over the cliff-like area, I felt the bones align back into their proper place. There was no longer any protrusion, just a solid bone and muscles.

I resumed moving my hands down the leg over the next comminuted fracture. When my palms covered the infirmity of the leg, that next fracture healed to become a solid bone. With the enthusiasm of what the Lord was doing running through me, I could barely contain myself to finish. Then proceeding to the final rupture as my palms covered that area, I could have sworn it seemed as if the man had gotten a little taller. Then my hands reached the ankle area. I retraced my steps moving my hands up and down the leg three times in different positions confirming there were no longer any breaks and no indication of any type of fracture. I raised his pants leg to see that the skin and muscles had the look of an athletic leg. I thanked Jesus and asked the Holy Spirit to fill any empty places. The man left, walking straight, with a smile from ear to ear. This healing ignited me with a fire I did not know I could achieve, and I did not stop any more in praying for others. It took a word from the Lord to my wife to keep me on track, and it still does today.

EVOLVING

Looking back, I can see that this work done by the Holy Spirit is very similar to man's attempts at healing through the radiations from Gama to X-ray. The major difference is the Holy Spirit side effects leave the person filled with love, joy, and peace and empowered to heal others with the same infirmities. This paradox is an extreme miracle and wonder of the gifts of healing. That is I, being able to see it and touch it, am a part of the treatment. Having the tools through my hands enabled by a touch of the Holy Spirit, I become the hand of God.

Little by little, like stepping stones, we are now being trained for the day when we as a people can harness the elements without mechanical augments. This gifting is part of the essence of the Kingdom. Both are evolving—the ability to accomplish miraculous results scientifically as well as supernaturally. We are just beginning to comprehend the bits and pieces of what awaits us—the greater works He said we would do. To me, that is the challenge—to step out with the Spirit and with Christ—and what fun it is!

Write down some of the unsolved mysteries you have encountered through your life no matter how small or mysterious. Then ask God to show you how you can become His hand in this.

Stadium Crusade

This paralyzed man's first steps. Thank you, Jesus!

My team's last event in Brazil would be to travel with Bill and Carol Dew to a village. Randy was preparing to leave the next day with team two for more crusades in other cities throughout the country.

That afternoon we had lunch together at a Brazilian restaurant located on a mountaintop overlooking the city of San Pablo. While sitting at the table looking out the window, I was taken into a trance. Being aware of my surrounding, I was not able to do anything except repeat a phrase declaring that witches and warlocks would come to know the glory of the God and give their lives to the Lord. In the vision, I saw silver, books, and other objects being burned, as adults and children were being set free and saved. I finally came out of the trance and fell into a slumbering state for almost an hour.

Evening came quickly as we were preparing to go to the village church. During the team ministry time, we were praying for those in need of healing. Brian was having difficulty with something interfering with the healings he was praying for. As he looked across the room, he saw a group of people pointing and speaking things at him. So he commanded them in the name of Jesus to be still, be quiet, and not to move. Instantly they became like statues—motionless and quiet, unable to do anything! When he had finished the healing work, Brian released those frozen across the room. Later that night, after they saw the true power of God, those four people who were witches and warlocks gave their lives to Christ.

I reflected back on the trance earlier that day on the ride to the village, thinking about the promise of what would occur. The simple truth is it will happen, but the question is when? Just as my lunch-time trance was manifested in the natural, so do other visions, dreams, and translations. The revelation awaits its appointed purpose in time. Don't you just love the way the Spirit moves?

AWAITING ITS APPOINTED TIME

On the bus ride to the village, I went into another vision. I saw myself walking down a road with others. There was a forest on my left side; on the other side of the road was an open field. I heard the instruction, *"Go into the woods."*

I pondered the jungle-like woods I saw before me in the vision. Then turning, walked into the woods as others followed me. Then after walking and talking for a while, suddenly in the middle of the woods was an open field that resembled a football/soccer field. I observed down the field some kids kicking a ball while others were riding bicycles. We continued walking as I scanned the scene before me. At the far end of the field was a house standing all alone. We walked to the house and knocked on the door.

To our surprise, answering the door was a little round man in his late fifties. Looking past the man into the home, I saw a woman sitting at what looked like a kitchen table. She stood up and came to the door. They spoke to each other for a moment as I turned to look at the field, asking questions of them and in my spirit. Then turning my attention back towards them, they smiled at me. We began to speak as everything vanished, and I found myself back on the bus.

This vision also is a stepping stone awaiting its appointed time for me and others, as its meaning is revealed later.

We returned from Brazil with our supernatural senses still on high alert—like the fishes coming out of the river into the aquarium. It was like keeping a headset over your ears for an extended period of time—your ears begin to adjust to that sound frequency and tone.

After returning to work, Pascal Bravo, a past client who knew I was going to Brazil on the mission trip, stopped by the office. He inquired how the trip went, asking if anything unusual happened. I gave him details and testimonies of what God was doing in Brazil. Pascal said that on the way to work one morning, the Lord told him to start praying for me right then and there, and he pulled off the freeway onto the shoulder of the road. He told me that he kept praying until the Lord had him stop. We thanked the Lord for watching out for us both.

CHRONICLES of A SEER

Team 1 & 2

Yes, I tell you, this generation will be held responsible for it all. Woe to you experts in the law, because you have taken away the key to knowledge. You yourselves have not entered, and you have hindered those who were entering. Luke 11:51-52

I say we are no longer ignorant as we are given knowledge, gaining experience, moving forward, and attaining wisdom to give counsel and understanding through the fear of the Lord. As for my children not knowing the truth that sets one free, the buck stops with me.

Chapter Thirteen

QUICKENING

A COUPLE OF MONTHS had passed since going to Brazil, and I had a compelling urge to attend the annual Voice of Apostles (VOA) Conference held every November. It was during the first evening of the conference that mysterious supernatural things happened. We were sitting with Tom and Dottie Hargest, among others from the Brazil team, who were also attending this conference. The technical department was having problems with the overhead projection system during the announcements. While waiting on the projector and PA system to be fixed, Randy Clark was loudly voicing the announcements. There was a tsunami that had hit India that previous year leaving great devastation in that country. Randy expressed that help was needed for India not only for the Healing Crusade in January, but also for food and clothing and other needs. Lorrie stepped out of the room at this point, and I sat talking with others as Randy paused during the announcements.

Tom and Dottie asked me if I was going to India, "I am not saying, 'No,' but I have no feelings whatsoever about going to India," I replied. "I would go if the Lord told me to go." I knew better than to say a straight "no." Sitting on the fence is not how you grow, which I would soon learn more about. That very next moment, the PA system began working as Randy said again, "I need help for the India trip." Instantly following that comment from Randy, *I got hit in the stomach by an unseen force, knocking the wind completely out of me and leaving me gasping for air.*

Nothing and no one was in front of me that I could see. Trying to figure out what had just happened, I heard Randy announce once again his need for help in India. Slam! I got hit in the stomach a second time. In between breaths, I heard Dottie and others saying, "You are going to India, aren't you"?

Just as I was about to answer, Randy broadcast through the PA system, "The India clip is ready." As he again spoke the word "India," I was hit again with a light force, being very thankful that the blow was not as powerful as the first one that got my full attention. I shook my head up and down as I blurted out , "Yes," between breaths. Then I heard one of my friends say, "We thought so."

Lorrie returned, and someone asked her if she was going to India. She looked at them, paused a moment as if listening, then responded with "No." Someone said to her, "Your husband is going," and she replied, "the Lord didn't tell me to go." This Holy-Spirit quickening distracted me for the remaining few days of the conference. I thought of what was going on in India and of my business with eight employees. My reasoning was, *this is not a wise business decision.* I considered how much it would cost.

Being owner of the corporation and its main source of revenue, I was considering the loss of potential future revenue and clients if I should be absent at this particular time right after the holidays.

"How often is God's will manifested on a person like this?" I asked, He answered, "Since you were not listening, I had to get your attention.

I also reflected on the fire of God that was released through the team in Brazil–how we dove in and did not sit on the sidelines.

My thoughts floated to people I would meet and the stories I would tell to them of Indian adventures. I knew I would experience wisdom, knowledge, and understanding that you cannot get from books, and that there would be transformed lives which you can't put a price tag on, only.

As I walked through the lobby where the resource tables were, I was intrigued by five books that contained the life story of William Branham. The back cover described him as a healing evangelist at the turn of the 20th century. It stated that this man was assigned an angel at birth by God for a destiny that would await him in signs and wonders. This angel had made many physical appearances one of which was photographed by a journalist as William baptized converts in a river. I bought the books at the conference and headed back to California to get ready for India.

INDIA

January came quickly with a 23-hour flight to Hyderabad, India. The team members were arriving from various locations around the globe through the night. I was shuttled to the hotel through 45 minutes of bumper-to-bumper traffic at one in the morning and checked into my room about 2:00AM.

The very first morning, the team was gathering in the lobby at 10:00 AM with our gear loaded on the bus and ready to be on the road by 11:00 AM. It was in the lobby that I saw four young women standing together. I heard the Voice give each of them a name that defined their character.

The first woman, though her real name was Danielle, was identified by the Voice as *Esther and Ruth*. The second young lady, Laura, was called Mary Magdalene. Sarah was named Joan of Arc, and the fourth young lady, Jackie, had an illuminating heavenly glow residing around her. I went over to introducing myself to see what the Lord was up to but got nothing at that time.

THE QUESTION ASKED AND ANSWERED

Jackie came up to me a couple of days later with some questions. "The Lord told me to ask you for my answers," she said, but she would not tell me what her questions were. She wanted answers for questions she put before the Lord. I looked into her eyes, but my sight was being withheld. I responded, "I have no answers for you at this time, but I will seek the Lord on what you are seeking me answers for."

This prompted my thoughts to the story of King Nebuchadnezzar where Daniel was required to interpret the king's mysterious dream with no clues to work with. In Daniel 2, the king had a dream and would not give the wise men the details of the dream in order to interpret its meaning. This king was going to kill all wise men in the country if none could tell him the dream and its meaning. Then Daniel, a man of God, told the king he would inquire of God for the dream and its interpretation. This challenge Jackie put before me pulled me in a direction which I had never gone before and created an upward stepping stone drawing on my shield of faith much like Daniel as he sought answers for Nebuchadnezzar.[38]

Early the next morning, I had a vision of Jackie fighting in a battle, along with others, against a common enemy. Jackie was not pleased with the way she was fighting and had many concerns. She knew there were many people watching and relying on her. She had been given a sword but was not using it properly; she was just holding it as if the sword was for looks only.

In the vision I said to her, "Use the sword." She looked at me with curiosity, pondering what to do. Then taking hold of the sword with a firm grip, she began to wield it; the sword led her in movement. She was now banishing the enemy with ease, being guided by the sword itself in each direction that she needed to go. With that, the vision was over.

But the Helper, the Holy Spirit, whom the Father will send in my name, he will teach you all things and bring to your remembrance all that I have said to you. (John 14:26)

It was later that morning that I ran into Jackie and her husband as they were talking to other people. I went over to them and gave Jackie the questions and answers she had inquired of the Lord. Jackie stood there a moment in amazement and then said, "I know these answers to my questions are from the Lord. It was all about the Sword of the Lord."

Quickening

We spent the rest of that morning talking about the Sword. Throughout the trip she would find me and ask more questions about the Sword that she didn't understand. In time, I directed her back to the Lord.

Let me backtrack a little on that first day in the city of Guntur. Early in the morning, I was sitting with Doc and Ed and a few others at the breakfast buffet in the hotel lobby when the ladies sitting with us excused themselves to get ready for our departure to the crusade. Within what seemed like a few minutes, Aney came bursting back into the breakfast room in a panic saying her roommate Suzie had fainted.

Ed and I, along with others, raced with Aney to her room located on a lower level. Aney pointed to her door down the hall on the left. I reached the door first, turning the unlocked door knob and pushing it open. As I stepped into the room, I was shoved to one side and pinned against the door by a huge, mystical matrix of shadows. I saw this shadow hunch over as it bolted out the door. It was a good thing Aney had stayed in the hall. The other guys jolted past me to aid Suzie. Shaken and puzzled as to how she ended up on the floor, Suzie assured us she was fine.

I, however, was angered by whatever that was from the mystical realm that knocked me flat! I stepped out of the room and looked up and down the hallway. I saw nothing but felt the unclean presence close by. When I told Ed, one of the leaders, that I actually felt something come out of the room and push me aside, Aney and others did a spiritual cleaning of the room, and things went back to normal.

The rest of that day continued with the team instrumental in praying through many healings at the pastors and leaders' meetings.

THE EVENING CRUSADE

The time came for the evening crusade. The head intercessor on this trip was Wendy Russell, an attorney from Texas. The intercessory team stayed on the bus while the rest of the team moved to the seating area on the side of the stage and Randy was waiting to be introduced. I was looking out the bus window curious to see what was happening when I saw Randy as a burning bush sitting in his chair writing things down. Then the Lord said to me, "Go over to the fence." I explained this to Wendy and asked to be excused from the intercessory team. She said to me, "Tell Randy what you saw." I went over and sat next to Randy, waiting until he responded, and shared with him what I saw. "I saw you as a burning bush, not being consumed though. Just as the Lord was with Moses on the mountain, so too, He will be with you."

He replied back to me, "I needed that. Thank you."

Earlier, while I was still on the bus, I had also observed a tornado touching down in different places of the fairgrounds where people were standing during the worship time. This tornado was expanding and contracting, and in each case, the tornado hit on the ground." This I also told to Wendy.

I walked over to the fence area as God had directed me and glanced over the size of the crowd. People were still coming in by the hundreds. I stood observing, waiting on the Lord to see what He was up to. Then something caught my attention. When my insides quieted down, and I again heard the words, "Go over to the fence." I looked at the fence from one end to the other and walked over to a particular area of the fence to look around.

The Voice quieted every sound around me, "Move over a couple of feet." With this new directive, I moved over two steps to my left. Then I heard Him say, "A little more," so I shuffled a little more to my left. I stood waiting for the next instruction. As I stood there, I heard these words "Take my Sword and strike it into the ground."

I had been carrying this special spiritual Sword of the Lord from Brazil that was given to Bryan and me. I reached with one hand, then the other hand, pulling the sword out of the scabbard and holding it steady and ready. I turned the point towards the ground with both hands on the hilt and drove the sword into the ground. As I looked, my vision opened into the spiritual realm like a clear sunny day.

As I observed the blade penetrating deep into the ground, I saw it going through an outline of a massive, dark image of an angel lying face down on its stomach as if sleeping. It was completely black in dimensional degrees of blackness. The sword's point struck through what would be the creature's left shoulder blade which had a huge wing protruding from it. The sword penetrated where the heart would be and fastened him to the ground. There was a flash as my vision shifted back into the natural reality. I heard a screeching scream of agonizing pain, and then, silence.

The scream was punctuated by a literal tremor in the ground. Viewing the surroundings in the distance, I witnessed the buildings ever so slightly sway back and forth. As lights came on in most of the buildings, the distant hills rippled the earthquake throughout the region. This creature, I realized, was a ruler or prince being taken out with the Sword of the Lord. I stood there amazed at what had just happened, unaware of anything else taking place. I began to realize that this was another upward stepping stone. While I was standing there in wonder, Wendy, who had just gotten off of the bus with the intercessors, come over to me.

Randy was now on the stage speaking as Wendy said to me, "We will now see what those tornados mean." The first thing Randy said was, "I believe the Lord is moving right now." He began pointing to certain areas in the crowd announcing, "There is healing going on in that area from the Lord." He then pointed to another area announcing again, "There is healing moving over there." He continued announcing this as he pointed to all the spots where I saw the tornados touch down. Wendy said with a smile, "That is what your tornadoes are all about," and then she returned back to the bus with the intercessors.

This took me back to when Moses spoke to Joshua, telling him that God would go before the children of Israel and promised to be with them and not forsake them in the land promised. The things accruing were beyond any comprehension. Taking out the ruler or authority set the stage for Deuteronomy 31:7-8[44] and released Jesus' decree of "Greater things you will do."[45] There were thousands of healings from small to miraculous that night. Thank you, Jesus! Amen.

---

44 Then Moses summoned Joshua and said to him in the sight of all Israel, "Be strong and courageous, for you shall go with this people into the land that the LORD has sworn to their fathers to give them, and you shall put them in possession of it. It is the LORD who goes before you. He will be with you; he will not leave you or forsake you. Do not fear or be dismayed. "

45 John 14

I wondered how many events through life have had a numinous intervention.

It is here I began to realize we are all working together building up this body of Christ with each part doing its part to equip the saints. We are being released with the keys of knowledge that had previously been obscured. These things we had previously been disregarded to go after, but now we are responsible for them. This is a part of the foundation of the working ministry of Christ–it is not with words of emptiness, but with power and might of the Holy Spirit. It is each of us responsibly using our gifts to encourage each other as we walk in faith.

This release left me feeling like The Pow, The Zip, The Zam, The Zowie of the old Batman and Robin movies. Having a Holy Spirit release of true authority and power had now become real.

This adventure with the Lord's Sword is one of the keys needed when entering into the mystical realms.

TRUMPETS LEADING THE WAY

The next day, the team had the afternoon off for a day of rest and fun. The bus driver was assigned to take those who wanted to go to the shopping market after lunch. I decided to go shopping to buy a few things for Lorrie and friends.

As I stepped up onto the bus, my insides started going berserk like a rat in a cage on a spinning wheel going nowhere. By the third step, my stomach was churning as if the rat was eating my insides. Looking up, I noticed the two Hindu statues on the dashboard of the bus were lighted, and for the first time since coming on the trip, incense was burning in front of the statues. My internal organs were on a rampage, and I couldn't breathe.

I stepped off the bus, and my insides returned to normal. I tried again to get on the bus, but as soon as I took the first step up, it was as if I was being choked. To test it once more, I stepped off and again I was able to breathe. I observed others on the bus through the windows, and they all seemed fine, except they seemed a little edgy. I forced myself onto the bus as my internal fight continued, and took a seat close to the door. I felt like invisible hands were wrapped around my throat trying to choke me. The bus drove to the shopping market as the suffocating feeling continued—until I prayed and then it subsided.

Later I heard from Wendy that she and others had also felt uncomfortable on the bus and during the ride. There was also a strange disconnect from the heavenly realm after that.

We all returned from shopping with a couple of hours to spare before the night crusade.

When I got back to my room, I was in need of spending time soaking in the presence of the Lord. So, pulling out my MP3 player, I listen to worship music with prayer. It was then I went into a dream-like trance, and I saw myself doing a march around the team bus. Instantly I was out of the vision, and it was time to go catch the shuttle to the main hotel where most of the team was staying.

Quickening

I ran down to the lobby to catch the shuttle a little early, but the shuttle was already gone. No one was there. I knew then I had a job to do. Quickly thinking of how I was going to get to the main hotel before everyone left for the crusade, with my backpack on, I started jogging to the main hotel a mile away, hoping that I could remember the route. I arrived just as Ed was ready to load the team onto the bus. "Wait!" I yelled between breaths, "Before anyone boards the bus, the Lord told me to do a Jericho march around the bus seven times."

Looking through the bus door, I saw the statues lighted with incense burning on the dashboard again. Thinking, *You spirits want to rumble?* I reached into my backpack, took out a bottle of anointing oil, and put some on my finger tip. I stepped up inside the bus and made a sign of the cross on the dashboard with the oil, stepped back outside on the ground and made another sign of the cross on the right side of the bus door. In prayer, I bound all the unclean spirits inside and around the bus and claimed the bus in the name of Jesus Christ, and then followed with the Jericho march around the bus. I asked Ed to keep count of the laps as we prayed while the team was waiting to get on board.

When the march was finished, I stepped up on board the bus and immediately felt a difference in my body. I felt great! It was a "Holy Cow!" moment as Robin would say. The driver and his assistant, looking at one another, showed utter astonishment as they saw their statues where no longer lit.

The bus was pulling away, and the driver was forcefully pushing on the horn to get into traffic. But oddly, for the first time, the horn would not work. In India, not having a horn is like having no headlights at night. It is constantly needed to signal other drivers. It is a must to navigate through dense traffic.

Just then Lynn, another prophetic team member, proclaimed aloud that she saw angels on the roof of the bus who were blowing their trumpets as everyone was getting on board. Two others on the bus confirmed they saw the same thing. Then someone else shouted, "We have our horns!" The bus arrived at the crusade venue that night as vehicles in traffic made way for our vehicle at every turn. The angelic presence never left during those times. The statues with the burning incense, as well as the bus horn, did not work for three days until I prayed for their release. "Who's the man now!" I thought as I thanked the Holy Spirit for His demonstration of power.

The rest of stories that took place in the city of Gunter is so many that I could write another book called the *Testimonies of Christ* filled with all the miraculous things that the Holy Spirit did through everyone on the team.

Other measures will be released as you will see in the other cities of India.

RAJAHMUNDRY

The team then arrived in Rajahmundry after three days in the city of Gunter. I was asked to lead the first morning's intercession sessions. Sharon, an intercessor, shared that she felt a Jericho march was needed around the tent where the pastors and leaders were in session.

The group acted on this and did a one-time march around the tent. The intercessor group felt a march was also needed around the crusade grounds that were being set up in an area about 200 yards away. During the march, we stopped to clean and anoint the corners with water and with anointing oil. I heard the Lord say, "Plant my Sword in this corner of the ground." Not wanting to leave this awesome sword that was given to me in Brazil, but knowing I had to, I pulled the Lord's sword out of the scabbard.[46] With both hands, turning and pointing it to the ground, I thrust it into the ground. I was remembering the legend of the sword Excalibur that was planted in a rock for only the true king to

---

46 Chapter 11 "The Awakening"

remove. The true king would return to take back his lands that had been stolen. After I removed my hands from around the hilt, I heard, "I will send someone to retrieve it one day."

This was the Lord telling us that He is taking back His land that had been stolen and has established anointed ones for this continent.

Now here is a paradox to think on: the carriers of His swords yield the Lord's swords when directed wherever we go. It is the presence they carry that translates His sword to them and leaves it in its designated place at the same time.

Then one of the intercessors heard the word "communion" as we were standing in the corner where the sword had been planted. Having only a honey oat granola bar between us, a team member, David, broke it into pieces in the wrapper. Each individual in the group prayed as led by the Holy Spirit, using water to represent the wine and the palm of their hand as a cup.

This was a night of great angelic activity in the heavens and on earth with signs and wonders manifested through every person on the team.

The next morning as the leader's conference was in session, I looked out the bus window while in a period of group intercession. The intercessors where charged and full of energy. Many had visions that needed to be released. Telling them, "Not yet," would be like trying to take the sugar out of a kid who has already eaten a box of cookies. We decided it was time to get off the bus and put everything given into action. The intercessors saw spiritual wells around the conference tent. We also saw a couple of dark grey areas about one foot in diameter in an almost all-white area of rocks. Something was different about the grey rocks as they actually became darker in the natural as we looked at them. We decided to pray over those grey areas while pouring bottled water over them for purifying, and then follow up by marching the entire grounds. Upon returning, we noticed that the grey areas had become all white like the rest of the rocks. Cool! While we were inquiring about this, we found out that people had been murdered in those very areas.

We learned this crusade location was a retired military base. While the leaders' teaching sessions were being held in a tent behind an old barracks next to a beat up old helipad, I was examining the pad, seeing something very transparent. As I prayed, focusing on the transparency, I saw what began as a stairway then became like a ladder before it vanished into the sky. Angels were ascending and descending upon it. I saw angels going both ways at the same time--one angel with his hand on a rope descending and another being pulled up with filled containers.

I said nothing about my vision but asked if anyone else saw anything on the helipad. Then as they were turning to walk away, one of the intercessors said, "I see angels appearing." With this confirmation revealed, we shared what I saw going on in this area with the angels. As I scanned the military grounds, I began to describe the types of angels that I saw as others who saw them did the same.

Behind the tent to the rear was a staging area of warrior angels. Some were on chariots in this one area. Some stood on tanks. Others stood on armored vehicles, jeeps, and troop carriers. To see the work being done in the hidden realm excited us like kids in a candy store. As we talked, others' eyes were opened to see what we saw and beyond[47]. It was what I call a rock-n-roll extravaganza of angelic activity that embodied us as we watched.

In another area, not far from where the grey spots had been on the white rocks, was the staging area for ministering angels with chariot-like wagons full of medical supplies and parts. Then separated from them to their right were healing angels with boxes that looked like gifts. There was another area on the other side of the tent where angels that I was not familiar with were unique with

---

47   2 Kings 6:17

boldness. Not knowing what kind of specialized angels these were, I was asking the Lord under my breath, but got no reply. How can one not long to join in with angelic presence when they manifest in this way? We were drawn like magnets to their personification of Christ Jesus. All that was left was to continue in prayer for this great release of the Kingdom.

I found out the next year what we saw was prophesied about Rajahmundry on August 20, 2006, on the Elijah list. The article was "The Chariots of God Have Been Released" by Kathie Walters.[48]

To me it is funny that we were in the exact place where it all was happening. Did we as intercessors help to bring it all about? It makes me wonder and want to ask the Father when I see Him, "What other roles did we all play in the unseen realms in different seasons of time?" What transpired there conveyed a better understanding of the roles of the angelic hosts in partnering with us to do the will of the Father. Oh, what a legacy we will have to tell our children and grandchildren of taking out unclean spirits and helping to set a country free! It not only relates to people, but also to cosmic powers, spheres, territories, regions, and animals.[49]

Below is an email that Suzie sent to me after returning from India. It is about the ordeal in the Guntur hotel with the unclean spirits.

"Thank you, Ramon, for the experience you had and the insight into what you felt as you entered my hotel room to help me out of my fainting ordeal. Actually, from what you shared about something coming out of the room and almost knocking you over, I realized the real truth about what happened. All along, I knew that the enemy was behind this attack (a concussion resulted). But now I know that I was pushed by an evil spirit, and was pressed down onto the floor till you all came into the room to

---

48 *www.elijahlist.com/words/display_word.html?ID=4400.*
49 Ephesian 6:12, Luke 11:24-26

'rescue' me. The enemy will do whatever he can to put down the saints of God and hinder the work God has for us. Thank you, along with the others, for being there and ministering to me.

God bless you mightily, as you serve Him in His Kingdom!"!

Suzie

Chapter Fourteen

A NEW COVERING

THE NEXT YEAR, LORRIE and I joined other ministry teams. If you want life adventures while finding out who you are in Christ, join outreach ministry teams. Trips to India increased dramatically and there was one particular trip where a divine Holy-Spirit connection was brought between the leader of India Christian Ministries (ICM) and me. Things exploded between us, as you will see. Later, after being rocked on a South Africa mission trip, pieces of this puzzle were coming together.

A few months after returning from India in 2007, I joined a Toronto Airport Christian Fellowship and Catch the Fire team led by Vicki Arnott that was headed to South Africa. This itinerary included traveling to Mozambique to minister with Iris Ministries run by Rowland and Heidi Baker who are known for moving in signs and wonders. The trip transformed my heart and brought me a great love for the team members—a very deep bonding known in Greek as *koinonia*. It just broke my heart when the journey was over. From the day the first team member headed home until I said farewell to the last, I found myself trying to hide my tears. This new love covers all people of all nationalities and cultures.

Revelation of the Father's heart for us all was expanding in me and through me as it will you. The greater wisdom of family was transforming my mind, heart, and spirit as never before. This Father's love is the crucial part of the healing process. Compassion moves the Holy Spirit when He is not moving. This release of compassion flows through you to the Father and back as Holy Spirit is moved by Father and healing is released. The characteristic heart of the Father in deeper relationship is a key to bringing personification of His heart. I saw this clearly released and evident in South Africa. We also had practical training in bush ministry through observing everything as well as being thrown into it—much like I did in the Marines. We dealt with witchcraft throughout the night with watchmen posted for guard duty and prayers. This brought angelic warriors to watch over the team as they slept. Their presence was captured by two different cameras just before dawn. It has been revealed through science that photos containing spheres like these viewed through certain lenses show the outline of what is believed to be an angel.

God stirred in me to bring a team to India in November with a similar pattern and agenda to what Randy and Vicki had with their teams.

A New Covering

The pictures tell the story as I jump back to India.

I sent out invitations to those I had traveled with on other mission trips in the past. We received donations in many forms, from monetary to spiritual seeds, that would be used for planting, watering, and harvesting of laborers for the great harvest. The monetary blessings went to some of the pastors to expand their ministry for much needed items for the community. In remote villages of great need, ICM was able to buy large quantities of food, clothing, and other necessities to distribute, particularly to orphanages and child development centers.

The last week of this trip would be a three-day pastors and leaders conference during the day and healing crusades at night. With hundreds of deities in India, many came to see if God was real. Here they found that God was real as the Holy Spirit *was* released mightily through the team.

And my speech and my preaching was not with enticing words of man's wisdom, but in demonstration of the Spirit and of power that your faith should not stand in the wisdom of men, but in the power of God.[50]

These excursions brought all involved to new levels of expectancy in belief and faith.

David and Beverly Huddleston out of Nova Scotia, a couple I traveled with earlier that year on the CTF South Africa trip, responded to my invitation to join the mission team for India. David was a retired Canadian fighter pilot commander and Beverly was a retired grade school teacher. Others who came were Mark West and Wayne Covington from The Mission. Wayne had a dream from the Lord that he was to go and capture these encounters on film. It was astounding and unbelievable that the team now had a film maker bringing his talents and equipment to document what would happen on this mission trip. Mark, a former youth minister out of San Francisco, is a businessman. It was funny how the Lord highlighted Mark out to me and me to Mark. "A match made in heaven," as they say. The mission trip would be twenty-five days, and Mark would connect up with the team two weeks into it. Mark's stories can be found in *Seers in the Kingdom: (Their Stories).*[51]

We experienced God's great favor months before the trip. While communicating with James, attention was brought to the fact that the equipment they rented for the events in India was old and unreliable. I decided to purchase the equipment and carry it over on the flight. I had no idea what was good, sturdy, and reliable equipment, nor how to make sure everything would actually work on the higher voltage system of India, or in the sand and extreme heat of 120 degrees Fahrenheit. In my research, I was able to narrow down the equipment that was needed with the help of my two friends, Wayne and Dan. I purchased a portable sound system, speakers, reversible viewing stadium screen, DVD player,

---

50   1 Corinthians 2:4-5.
51   Seers in the Kingdom (Their Stories) can be bought www.Amazon.com.

projector, microphones, stands, and backup power supply as well as a compact travel case large enough to carry everything. Making this decision that whatever I buy, it would be as if I was buying it for myself or my family following my strict personal principle, "The Golden Rule."[52] I decided we would leave the equipment with ICM so they could continue with their calling.

LISTENING

In preplanning the costs, I called United Airlines for the shipping charges, since we would personally hand carry everything into the country with our luggage. The airlines gave me a quote over the phone of about $125, but I heard, "$1,192." I wasn't sure if what I was hearing was just my imagination, so the next day, I called again and received the same dollar amount. *That is less than two hundred US dollars!* I said to myself. *I must have heard the other quote incorrectly yesterday.*

Our big day came, and we were departing out of the San Francisco International Airport. We checked in at the United Airlines Premier Executive counter with all of our equipment and luggage. The UA check-in agent finished weighing everything and said, "That will be an extra $1,500 for over-the-limit weight."

I stood there in shock. Here I was only expecting about $250 dollars maximum. I said to the agent, "I believe you are wrong," and then explained that I had called to check the cost twice and was told that it would be only from $125 to $250 dollars for the extra weight.

Soon the airlines supervisor came over to see what was going on. We each explained the situation and the supervisor said to me, "Let me take a look at this." While she was working on getting everything in order, Wayne happened to notice that the supervisor's name tag read "Lord." I pulled Wayne over to the

---

52 The Golden Rule: "So whatever you wish that others would do to you, do also to them, for this is the Law of the Prophets." Matthew 7:12.

side and explained to him I had supernaturally heard $1,192 dollars on the phone when I had first called United for the equipment luggage quote. After a few minutes passed, we were called back to the counter and the supervisor said to me, "It will be $1,192." We looked at each other with astonishment. Just then Wayne says, "The Lord said $1,192, and we need to listen." I paid the fee.

A little disappointed in myself for not listening to what I had originally heard on the phone, I had to laugh at the humor of the supervisor's name, "Lord." With that, we boarded the plane for India knowing God has great sense of humor

Having arrived at the Mumbai International Airport, and getting through customs, we connected with the CTF team which also had arrived and was doing an ILSOM conference. We would be a part of their team for the first seven days then split off. This time with TACF was an incredible part of the journey which included receiving as well as impartation and ministry.

After our CTF time, we met up with Mark at the international airport in Hyderabad. The city of Hyderabad reminded me of Chicago back when I was a child. The ICM crew sent to meet us was Readi, Raju and Chicie-Baba with three SUVs perfectly suitable for rural travel. We had a six-hour drive south to the city of Ongole. It was a unique drive going through the country with the three vehicles: one carrying all the equipment and the other two vehicles with the luggage and team members. We arrived and checked into the hotel to get some much needed rest for the coming days' planned events.

THE ADVENTURES

Our first day began as we set out for the first village where we ministered and then set up to do a Jesus film. Wayne taught the ICM team how to set up and use the newly purchased equipment.

The film was being shown in the heart of the village, which we learned was mainly Muslim and Hindu with some Christians living in the outskirts of the village. The darkness crept in quickly as the area became packed with people. They were drawn in by the sound of the worship prior to the showing of the film "The Gospel of Luke" that played in Telugu, a major language in India. It told the story of Jesus and could be viewed on both sides of the screen. Those from the village could actually watch the film from their homes while looking out their windows and back doors, and some came outside to watch the film. Showing the film in this way reminded me of when I used to go to the drive-in theater.

At the end of the film, we gave a salvation call and about a third of the people stood up to give their lives to Christ Jesus. The team then moved into ministering healings after the first call of salvation, and signs and wonders followed in the power of the Word: deaf ears opened, a broken ankle was healed, ligaments that had been torn or damaged were repaired, swellings disappeared, various pains healed, and sight was restored to a person who was going blind. Thank you, Jesus, for what You have done and will do.

As the team moved from village to village over the next week, these miracles continued. We visited the local pastor's home and child development centers which were run by the church and which provided the children with a nourishing meal and education each day while also teaching about the love of the Father.

In one village, the pastor's wife had just given birth to a baby boy. The wife resembled a cousin of mine, Tammy Pina, so much I thought they could be twins! The pastor with his wife asked me to be the godfather of their newborn and to name the boy. Edison, our interpreter and a regional pastor, told me, "This is an honor for them to have you name the child." I gave the baby the name Josiah. They had already chosen Daniel as the first name, so he became Daniel Josiah. There was a big smile on the parents' faces as Edison translated it with the biblical reference. I picked Josiah because he was the good king, walking in the ways of the Lord,[53] which brought an even greater smile to the other family members who were there listening. This godfather-thing resonated in me as I was also the godfather of Tammy's daughter, Kaelyn. It makes you wonder as you see the joy in such tangible ways that comes out of following your calling.

Daniel Josiah

It was now time for the pastors and leaders conference in Ongole. The first night of the healing crusade, I got this overwhelming feeling of joy during the worship as I was sitting in a chair waiting on ministry time. I just stood up and started dancing my way up the stage platform without concern of dignity and just continued jumping and dancing in the joy I was receiving. There was a release of freedom in the air as I continued dancing on the platform. After the heavy presence on me resided, I stepped down off the stage.

---

53 2 Kings 22, 23, 2 Chronicles 34, 35.

A New Covering

Children's Development Center

It was time for ICM to introduce me along with Edison my interpreter. The atmosphere started getting electrified into Actual encounters; my sight was released to see what was happening in the spiritual world. The only words that would come out of my mouth were "Jesus" as the translator repeated. Looking at everyone again, I yelled, "Jesus!" with the translator following me and my actions. The crowd yelled back, "Jesus!" Then I did it a third time, "Jesus!" but before the interpreter could even finish saying "Jesus!" the crowd began to respond with great joy to His name.

This happened two more times and the crowd got louder and louder as electricity was flowing through the air the size of lightning bolts. It was then that I saw the heavens breaking open. I paused and observed what I was seeing over the crowd. I saw a cloud form in an area over the people to my right. I knew by this sign that Jesus was healing people in that area. I could see a misty something hovering over them. Edison followed me, announcing what I saw and spoke out. I pointed as the cloud shifted over the people and as the healing power of Jesus was moving over the people. I knew then Jesus was going straight into healings and that the sermon I had prepared would follow afterwards. I began to say to the crowd, "If anyone is feeling anything happening in their body, such as heat, electricity, coldness—anything different—stand up. A majority of people began to stand in the area under the misty cloud I had seen and in other areas where Jesus was healing them. Thank you, Jesus. Amen.

At this point, Mark came up on the stage and joined me with words of knowledge. I handed him the microphone. Turning back to the crowd, I could see the cloud was moving to my left to the back of the crowd. I announced, "If you feel anything happening in your body, stand up." There was a man who had a tumor the size of a grapefruit on his underarm standing up. He was feeling something—the tumor from his underarm fell off to the ground! The skin of his underarm where the tumor fell off had been all white and pink. It had now healed so completely that it returned to his natural brown color.[54]

Mark gave the words of knowledge that he was receiving, asking those people in the crowd to stand who had the symptoms that he called out.

"Jesus wants to heal you, and standing up is an act of belief," he shouted. As they were standing, Jesus healed them of their infirmities as Mark gave thanks to Jesus. There were hundreds of healings that day as we cursed aliments, injuries, and cancers. The man healed from the tumor, brought the tumor to the front of

---

[54] This report we heard in a manner of minutes from those standing next to him.

the stage and left it on the ground at the end of the night before leaving. Take that to the bank on who Jesus is!

How can a person say there is no Jesus or God to a person who has just been healed or to the person is who has witnessed a miracle take place? We thanked the Lord for allowing us to make a difference in that person's life. You see we didn't believe the lie that Jesus doesn't do miracles, signs, and wonders anymore. *He is the same yesterday and today and forever.*[55] We went after the knowledge that was withheld.[56] I said to the crowd, "Always give thanks to God, no matter how small." The word spread and the crusade grew those three nights. There were about 1,500 people who came the last night to see and learn about Jesus.

The twenty-five days came to an end, and we were all sad to have to leave our new family. Because we had experienced such koinonia fellowship together, we decided to return as a team again the following year to continue what God started in us and in India.

I continued traveling the globe, joining other teams, igniting fires by the releasing of the Father's love for all. I stayed the course for India in 2008. It was when I was planning to lead a team to India in 2010 that I felt the call was being redirected to South Korea and to Afghanistan. More keys, stepping stones, beacons, and markers to prophecies that where given from decades past became like a compass heading which brought pieces of a puzzle to form a map to the next destination.

---

55 Hebrews 13:8

56 "You're hopeless, you religion scholars! You took the key of knowledge, but instead of unlocking doors, you locked them. You won't go in yourself, and won't let anyone else in either." (Luke 11:52, MSG)

Wayne and ICM team

Team India 2007

Chapter Fifteen

STEALING

HAVING BEEN BACK HOME a few months, I tore a muscle and/or ligament in my thigh. The Lord healed it after I laid hands on my thigh and prayed. Two weeks later, I was relaxing at home with Lorrie and Josiah as we watched a movie together. I was sitting on the floor stretching during the movie when, all of a sudden, I heard what sounded like the crashing, crunching, and crackling of about a dozen knuckles being cracked all at the same time.

The sound came from the top of my knee and up the inside of the leg muscle to the groin. It was followed by a rush of swelling and pain. I was not able to lift my leg. I knew of no bones in that area. There are multiple muscles, ligaments, and sciatic nerve that follow along that path. I tried to analyze what had just happened to no avail.

My first thought was, *Lord, You healed my leg two weeks ago, what is this?* My second thought was that the enemy was trying to falter my faith in healing by trying to pilfer the healing.

So, I decided to keep working the left leg using my hands to move the leg up and down, and everything started to work again. There was excruciating pain as I pressed through the torment. I went to bed after the movie and just kept thanking Jesus through the night as I slept, claiming the healing that was mine.

Getting up that next morning, most of the pain was gone. The inside muscles were all very tender and still swollen. I said to myself, *I am not going to be robbed of my morning routine of reading, soaking, and finishing it with a physical workout.* When it was time to work out, all I could accomplish was leg lifts with knees bent with the help of my hands pulling up and supporting the leg muscles. I kept claiming the healing in Jesus name that I had received weeks before. When I reached the 14th leg lift with the help of my hands, I said, "Lord, let's try 20..." and continuing working until I reached 20 lifts. With persistence, I said, "Let's keep going," as I pressed on to 30 lifts with no hands. I was not willing to quit, so I said, "Lord, 50!" The next thing you know, I was at 60 with legs straight and no hands as I finished with 120 leg lifts.

It was time for my morning run. Going outside and starting down the road, I was thinking if someone had a camera right now, they would have had a blast taking pictures for one of those hidden camera shows. The run was a cross between shuffle-scuttle and a hop as I reached the half-mile marker. I said, "Lord, we are in this together..." The next thing I knew, I was doing a normal jog, giving thanks along the way. *Thank you, Lord!*

When I got home after doing the two-mile jog, I decided to finish my workout in the garage with some rounds kicking on the heavy bag, doing five two-minute rounds. Then I tried some jump rope. With the first try at jumping rope, nothing seemed to work. With steadfastness, by the third try, everything was working together. This is *emunah*[57] to me—*let it be for me as you have said, Lord.*

> *Do not let the enemy steal what you have been given and the ground you have taken. Everything has been given to us.*[58]
> *It is yours and Satan will try to steal it, kill it, or destroy it.*[59]

This is an important part of the good fight.

---

57 Hebrew, word meaning "more than faith."
58 Luke 10:19 19, "Behold, I have given you authority over all the power of the enemy, and nothing shall hurt you."
59 John 10:10.

CALI, COLUMBIA & INDIA

Looking for more adventures, Lorrie and I joined Bill and Carol Dew's team to Cali, Colombia, in South America. We saw hundreds of signs and wonders unfold before our very eyes. One such wonder was the healing of a severely ill infant. The pastors from Colorado, Patricia and Fred Bruener, saw a mother holding her baby with greenish colored skin and an extremely high temperature in the market place. Some of the areas of the infant body were swollen. The Brueners went with the interpreter to seek permission from the mother to lay hands on and pray for the baby. They were given permission, and laid hands to pray for the infant while the other team members joined in. The Lord released instant healing as everyone watched the transformation into a perfectly healthy baby. That is what you call a WOW moment. I wondered what those shoppers thought about that; we gave thanks to Jesus. That was a birthday my wife and I will never forget.

Stepping our story up into India 2008, the plan was to spend a week with the CTF team as we did before and then again to do an ILSOM in Hyderabad. The rapidly declining global economy had changed my plans, and I had to shorten my time away from the office. The office staff now consisted of only one employee. I arrived three days late and just in time for the closing of that night's event at the ILSOM conference. John Arnott was sitting there listening to that night's speaker. When the speaker had finished, John proceeded to do the closing and tying up of any loose ends by referencing Scriptures on what the speaker had just taught.

Just before this, I was standing in the back of the room watching old friends from the previous year's trip to Mumbai taking part. The senior leader from the Mumbai conference saw me standing in the back of the room. He came up, gave me a hug, and then took me to a seat in the second row behind where John was seated, moving another person who was sitting there directing him,

"Please sit here." I was then welcomed with honors by John Arnott as he was doing the closing of that session. John, when closing, brought greater revelation to the teachings of the one who had spoken that night. John's analogies of the Scriptures in closing were exceptional, as I have never heard anything less from him. I was glad to be able to hear John close as it was a new learning experience for me. I had never heard anyone close a teaching the way John did that night. I was listening to a founding father setting the groundwork for the release of supernatural encounters. I wished everyone could hear him speak.

This reminded me of how I faltered in doing my first closing in the Philippines. I learned now from a father figure how to do it right. The next evening, John closed the event in the unique fashion of a fire tunnel such as I had never seen before. The tunnel was self-propelling until the time when we were ready for it to stop. I decided I would use this same tunnel in the two-day leader's advance that my team would be speaking in. I watched a wave of fire encompass the leaders there. The last two days went by quickly, now being time to depart from the CTF team. Team India would start the next day with the rest of the team members flying into Hyderabad.

Mark was flying in from the USA. David and Beverly flew in from another part of India, having been part of another CTF ILSOM. CTF had organized ILSOM's in ten different cities with ten different teams all at the same time! I felt this was a great accomplishment to spread the love of the Father by using teams since one person or team cannot accomplish so much alone. We heard the testimonies of how might and power followed the CTF teams at every location. It was now time for the six-hour drive to Ongole to start the second phase of adventures,

Ongole would be the home base of our outreach ministry to extremely remote villages. Excitement ran through me. We had seen on the news that missionaries had been killed a few weeks earlier further northwest from our location by Muslim and Hindu extremist. This location was keeping us a safe distance from the incidents. The closest village was three hours from Ongole with another two hours reach for other outlining villages from that point still keeping us a safe distance away from the tragedies.

TORMENTING SPIRIT

The team had been going from village to village ministering prayer for healing from house to house. We broke into two teams, each accompanied by a local pastor and interpreter. Beverly and David were one team, and Mark and I were another. Mark and I were walking side-by-side talking and admiring the different details of the village huts as we passed by them. Edison, who was the regional pastor and our interpreter, and the village pastor were leading the way. I noticed that three-foot-high pieces of bamboo stuck in the ground in perfect alignment. These were the markers to define property lines for each hut.

Then suddenly my head whips around from being slapped to the right side. Looking around but seeing nothing, I asked Mark, "Did you feel that?"

"No," he replied. "Why?"

"I just got slapped!" I replied.

Mark confirmed, "I saw your head get whipped around."

I turned, focusing on the houses in the direction from which the slap came. I stopped, now looking at one house. Going into a silent prayer, I asked the Lord, "What just happened?"

I heard Him say, "It is a tormenting spirit."

Thank you, Lord.

Then turning and looking at Mark, I repeated to him what I had just heard the Lord say, "It is a tormenting Spirit." We followed the pastor and Edison through the little bamboo gate into the yard, waiting as the village pastor went into the house. Following him out was a teenage girl holding a baby. I waited patiently, observing the girl as the village pastor was introducing everyone. I said to Edison after the formalities, "Ask her if she was being tormented by evil spirits."

The girl looked with astonishment and shock at Edison while he was speaking to her. As he finished, she responded, "No," which is easy to understand in any language. A few more words followed. Edison was translating the words she spoke into English as the senior pastor became very irritated. He turned to the girl speaking sternly in a nonstop tone.

Mark and I looked over at the village pastor then to Edison asking him what was going on? He sharply told us to be quiet so that he could hear. The pastor and the teenage girl were in heavy dialogue as Edison listened. When they concluded, Edison smiled asking how I knew as he relayed to us what had just transpired between the two of them. The senior pastor told the girl that her mother had been coming to see him for the last few months asking him to pray for her. The mother told him that her daughter was being tormented by evil spirits at night. The village pastor told her to stop lying and tell the truth.

I asked if we could lay on hands and pray for her and for the baby. She agreed, and we prayed for the girl and then for the baby girl she was holding. While rebuking the assignments of the tormenting spirits and binding those spirits, we realized they could not be cast aside at that time. It was not the right time to remove the root. Our efforts held a few of the tormenting spirits as we cast out the others. This concluded with a releasing of angelic protection over her and the household as we were led by the Holy Spirit. We invited her and the baby to the healing crusade that would take place in a couple of days. She told us she would not be able to make it.

We continued on to another area of the village. The next house had a woman waiting with her family wanting prayer. As soon as we laid hands in prayer on the lady, she was slain in the Spirit and collapsed straight to the ground. In this state, a person is in the actual presence of the Lord being ministered to by Holy Spirit and or by angelic hosts. As this woman lay there on the ground, I saw vapor, like waves, rising in the air and departing from her. We continued to lay on hands and soak her with the Presence. After about 20 minutes in the presence of God, she arose looking like a flower that had just blossomed. We continued on in this favor and grace as the village pastor led us all the way to the far end of the village.

Not all needs were health issues. There was one lady who was in desperate need of funds to pay a debt. We prayed for her to get the money needed to pay off what we would call a loan shark by the given deadline. The teams continued going from house to house. Some of the people were believers others were Hindus, but all were created by God no matter what religion. His grace and mercy were there with love.

I felt a sphere shift as the Holy Spirit began moving differently through me now in this village. The shift began in one particular hut where I stopped to pray for a family. My whole body started heating up like a teapot of water on a stovetop. I started conjecturing on what was happening. I realized that as I laid hands on the sick and the Holy Spirit moved through me, the steam would start pouring out of my pores from the top of my head to the bottom of my feet with electricity flowing from my hands. The people we laid hands on became completely healed in that village.

As we continued going from hut to house, I began to realize the greater the sickness or infirmity in the person, the more intense the steam and heat that protruded from within me. This greater outpouring of steam from my body caused me to become extremely thirsty. My body was in need of much water. I used up all the water in my backpack and my shirt became dripping with sweat as I continually wiped the sweat from my face. It was like I was running a marathon.

The people kept putting money in our hands and pockets as we went from place to place. There were some of the village ladies who lived further out that wanted prayer over the bottles of oil and articles of clothing they brought with them. They planned to take these items home to lay on those who needed to be healed. I didn't realize until later it might have been a good idea as in Acts 19 to wipe the prayer clothes with sweat as Paul did, but sweat got on the prayer cloths anyway since I was dripping everywhere!

Mark and I looked at each other in wonder at what the Holy Spirit was doing through the steam and electricity. The look on the people's faces told the story of a heavenly encounter. Edison asked us to pray for him also in between stops. People were staring in amazement at the outpouring of steam as we laid on hands in praying for the sick. That to me was a sign and a wonder pointing to God.

Mild illnesses such as headaches, swelling, and back problems didn't create much steam. However, I prayed for one older man who had back problems, becoming a boiling teapot as my insides whistled that it was ready to be poured out. While I was praying for his back, I stopped and then asked if he had any other ailments. The old man replied, "Yes," but he was more concerned with the back pain being gone so he could continue going to work. I love it when the Lord has other plans as the "Kingdom of Heaven is at hand."[60]

All the infirmities in the older man disappeared. A tumor disappeared and swollen internal organs no longer protruded from his body as they were healed. He stood up, no longer hunching over, and announced all pain was gone as he shifted and moved around while we witnessed his body realigning. The smile on his face was priceless, and he gave thanks to us and to Jesus as we all

---

60 Mat 10:7-8 The kingdom of heaven is at hand. 8 Heal the sick, raise the dead, cleanse lepers, cast out demons.

gave thanks to Jesus. The steam and electricity subsided from me letting us know our work was done.

From then on, when I asked a person if they needed prayer for anything, I could tell from the manifestation of steam and electricity the intensity or complexity of the healing needed. I was also becoming aware of certain types of infirmities without being told what they were. I was now receiving a word of knowledge of physical ailments through the steam and electrical currents. I would ask if what I felt was what they wanted prayer for and was accurate in naming the aliment.

In one such case I was getting the buildup of steam with words of knowledge in a vision. I could see the part of the person's body which had the infirmity, and then I knew how to pray for that illness.

These were the stepping stones for Mark and me for what was to come.

We approached a hut where a woman was lying on a hammock outside covered with a mosquito net. We were told by her mother and father that the woman had tuberculosis and AIDS. The woman looked as if these were her final days on earth. This, in my eyes, was a David-and-Goliath moment. I remembered that God promised He would go before us and be with us.[61] From a distance, Mark and I saw more than just frailties; there were also unclean spirits in and around her. We looked at each other, giving a nod that confirmed what each of us was seeing.

The mother went to her daughter stating we had come to pray for her and that we would lay hands on her. Then as we approached the daughter, the village pastor and Edison kept their distance. The daughter went ballistic on the hammock, trying to shuffle to the far end of the hammock away from us. We saw that the unclean spirits realized the Holy Spirit and Jesus were with us.

We looked at each other with another nod of our heads. I pulled out the anointing oil, pouring it onto our hands. We then

---

61 Deuteronomy 31:8

commanded the afflicting spirits to be still and to do no harm. We then commanded the unclean spirit to leave. She then lay calmly back in the hammock as we laid our hands on her head and feet and each took turns in prayer as led by the Holy Spirit. We spoke in tongues in between the commands of healing into her body in Jesus name.

The more we prayed, the more peace and calmness came over her. Her skin began changing from dried and prune-ish to smooth. Her muscles underneath re-energized, the wrinkles in the skin began leaving, and we saw strength return. The appearance of death was gone. She was becoming healthier and giving thanks. (To get a visual of what happened next, it was like the scene in the movie "*The Two Towers*" in the trilogy of "*The Lord of the Rings*" where Gandalf the White restored the King from being possessed by Saruman an evil spirit from sorcery.) This daughter was set free and restored. We thanked the Lord and continued on when the steam and electrical current resided.

The people never stopped sticking money in Mark's and my hands and pockets. We were told by Edison and the senior pastor to accept it so as not to offend the people. When it was time to leave, both teams took the money we had been given and put it in the hands of the local pastor. We asked him to give the money to the woman who needed money to pay the loan, and he agreed to do it. You see God answered everyone who stepped up and asked for prayer.

The testimonies of Jesus that came through the people had spread throughout the region. People traveled hours to come to the Jesus films. We were invited by multiple Muslim families to come to their homes and to lay hands on their family members for healings; the doors were opened for Jesus. It was now the last part of the trip with the healing crusade at night along with the pastors and leaders conference during the day. The pastors from ICM were watching everything that we were doing and sending reports back to headquarters and out to other villages. Many leaders came for the conference during the day. We found out that they ran out of food to feed all the leaders who came and had to go get more.

LEADERS AND CRUSADES

With the leaders, I shared the Transformation clip that was done back in the eighties on how Cali, Columbia, was transformed by grace as the people began giving their hearts to God. The film showed how the people began calling on God for help resulting in the land, the towns, and the cities being transformed into a prosperous healthy country. The land now produced resources it never had the capability to do before, and the scientific community could give no explanation. I told the people this is what God's miracles are for. God wants our children to prosper and grow together no matter what country we are in or language we speak as we unite in prayer. This is God's heart for India, and the rest of the world, that our children will grow together as we pave the road to transformation.

Pastors & Leaders Fire Tunnel of Imparation

The nightly healing crusade was set up on the outskirts of a major town which was another two hours away from where the pastor and leaders conference was being held during the day. This crusade did not feel even close to having the same experience in the spiritual realm as the year before. My seer vision was withheld. No, not withheld, but rather bound or constrained during the crusade nights I felt. It seemed that I was fighting against ignorant charismatic prayers of old. The crusade grounds were owned by an old Christian denomination. It was as if a prayer of old was keeping my abilities contained and what was needed was a breakthrough. There was a sermon given with some healings manifested, but the atmosphere was not ignited even though the crowd had doubled in size from the year before. We broke into individual ministry time as well with the laying on of hands for those who did not get healed during the sermon.

Healing Crusade

I said, "Lord we need the Holy Spirit. Please send more signs that the people could see Jesus is real and that they could see there is only one true God. They worship so many false gods, idols, and spirits in India. We are Yours. Thank you, Lord.

Then Mark, who was praying for people, started getting very excited. He had a person with a blind eye opened to perfect sight. The Holy Spirit was moving through him and around him. He was like a baseball player who just hit a home run. That excitement generated greater faith into the crowd. Beverly took a swing in praying for a person who was mute, and the Lord gave speech—another home run! These hits were announced over the PA system through the interpreters, energizing the atmosphere. Thank you, Jesus. We all began getting boxed in by people who needed healings. I sent a mute person to Beverly's line later that night. He was surrounded by his family who saw him learning to speak his first words. Is that a home run or what?

There were rivers of Living Water flowing out through the team as the might of the Lord moved.[62] There were at least a dozen mute people who received their speech as well as healing for all the other infirmities people had. Thank you, Jesus.

---

62 "Whoever believes in me, as the Scripture has said, 'Out of his heart will flow rivers of living water.'" John 7:38.

With rivers of healings, the corporate anointing was released. The local team leaders began laying hands on people, and anointing flowed through them for greater healings.

Then, as I was praying for a little girl, the Holy Spirit opened her ears instantly. Then looking down the line I saw that teenage girl with the tormenting spirit, along with her baby, whom we had prayed with at her home in the village earlier in the week. Here she was, wanting prayer. This sent a rejuvenation running through me. I quickly laid hands on those in line in order to reach her. Greater authority and power shot through me as I saw healings and unclean spirits taking flight in the spirit realm. The angelic hosts smiled, and that spiritual hindrance we encountered upon our arrival was no longer in the way. This is what "the Kingdom of Heaven is at hand" looks like. Disease and sickness cannot stand as joy, laughter, and peace become the theme in thanksgiving to Jesus. It is a wonderful thing to see the expression of a person who was made whole (*sozo*) when you prayed, giving praise to Jesus.

SUNDAY MORNING

The team was departing Sunday morning for Hyderabad right after the service. The vehicles had been loaded with the luggage, leaving behind the brand new equipment. The Ongole ICM pastor introduced me as the speaker. I shared events of the past week and the testimonies of what Jesus had done and was still doing. Then suddenly, the Holy Spirit redirected me to a different topic as I was speaking.

I paused for a minute or two waiting on the Lord. I let the crowd know that I was to speak on a different subject. I continued by telling some of the past events of my youth. I used my testimony as the focal point and analogy to give a greater understanding to what I was communicating. I began to refer to the caste system in India and referenced how each society throughout time has tried to maintain a type of caste system. Some places still do.

Like slavery in the USA until abolished, it was a principality allowed too reign. Its evidence was still strong even into the nineteen-sixties as prejudice continued to remain. This is a culture of life that can affect us all out of ignorance just as each person responds differently to the caste system in India. This caste system is just a tool and, if allowed to continue, will keep people in a place of control. I continued to speak of the wonders of God and how His love changed, and is changing, generations, removing these systems as we join together as brothers and sisters with one another.

I finished the sermon, and my emotions unfolded as I recalled the time when Lorrie's ex-stepfather believed in a caste-type system.[63] I turned the microphone over to Mark in closing. We prayed and laid hands on the congregation before heading to the airport after the service.

---

63 Chapter 5 Consequences with Favor

I realized then that these adventures were leading to an unknown destination for me, as well as others jumping on board, each were being prepared them for their own destinations and callings the Lord has for them.

Chapter Sixteen
A PROPHECY AND PROMISE

IT HAS BEEN A season of rest as the global economy has altered my income which in turn affected what I was able to do personally for missions. Even so, no matter what kind of season we are in, there are always testimonies of the Father's love. My own father, Raymond, always said to me, "Keep an open mind, but be strong-minded and a leader God bless you".

At Christmas time 2009, I attended a Christmas party where I heard that my friend Dan was preparing to go to South Korea in January 2010. He would be speaking at the C. Peter Wagner Leadership Institute (WLI). My heart and spirit leaped, and I knew I was supposed to go. Going back to the Orient had been in my spirit for the past year. I asked Dan if I could join him, and he replied, "I would enjoy the company." This time the obstacle that reared up was finances. I knew I had to take a step of faith. So, I took the last of our money we were using for the cabin and used it to make this mission trip. This cabin took everything we had from savings to retirement to build, leaving us broke. Sadly, we had been ripped off by a contractor during the building process, yet I asked myself how much did I want to fulfill a calling, even if not knowing or fully understanding? Thinking back on the epiphany I experienced which is described in chapter 9, *I will pay the price no matter the cost, I put my trust in you Lord,* I chose to invest in the calling.

We arrived in Seoul, South Korea, and were met at the airport by Charles of Harvest International Ministries (HIM). It was a 35-minute drive to the hotel. I observed spiritual atmosphere changes on the way, and mentioned what I saw. These changes had different levels of heavenly ambiance. Then as Charles drove out from a freeway tunnel and then crossed over a bridge, I had a delightful taste of honey in my mouth. I was telling Dan about the supernatural taste and the shifting of angelic authority in each of the regions that I saw as we drove. We arrived at the hotel and settled into our rooms. The next day came quickly.

There is favor and opportunity if you look for it and are willing to step into it. I was headed down to the lobby to meet our driver but decided to run back to my room to get an item I had forgotten. Getting into the elevator, I saw a very distinguished older man in an overcoat. I said a polite "Hello" as I stepped in. We struck up a short conversation until we each arrived at our respective floors. When I retrieved my stuff from my room and got back on the elevator, there he was again. During our second conversation, I found out he was the vice-president of this prestigious hotel chain in South Korea. We parted and went our separate ways again.

Again, while waiting with Dan in the lobby for our driver, the vice-president approached, and I introduced him to Dan. He asked who we were waiting for and how we liked South Korea. After a few minutes, he pulled out his phone he called HIM headquarters to ask if the driver was en route. Come to find out, he was personally acquainted with the senior leaders of HIM. He told us our driver would be there shortly as he climbed into his own waiting limo. Our driver pulled up shortly after that.

After arriving at one of the HIM churches, we were able to spend time getting to know the other leaders. We spent the next three days at that HIM church as Dan ministered and they allowed me the privilege of giving testimonies of what God had done through my life. Three days went by, and it was time to pack up and head into the country where the WLI was located for the week-long retreat of professors, doctors, pastors, leaders, and businessmen and women.

During our time at WLI, our prophetic ability was in high demand. At breakfast, lunch, and dinner, we would be joined by at least eight other leaders and businessmen or women. It was in these relationship-building settings that the unseen came to life. After prayer but before the meal was served, Dan and I were asked to prophesy over each guest at the table. Except for the four main pastors and leaders, there were different guests at each meal.

It was during one of these spectacular meals where we were being asked for prophetic words for the businesswoman who had joined us that I received a vision of a young man across the waters. When I finished revealing the vision, Dan interpreted parts of the vision. Then instantly, those sitting at the table pulled out their cell phones and started making calls. I wondered what was the Holy Spirit releasing and why? The next day it was announced during our lunch that the businesswoman had wire-transferred a donation equivalent to $100,000 US dollars into the HIM account. That was the first time I had ever seen anything like that happen as a result of a prophetic word of knowledge. This circumstance had definitely "wowed" me in the natural.

During a break time at WLI, Dan and I returned to the guest house to rest. I was on my laptop watching a podcast of Bob Jones speaking at Morningstar. Dan walked into the room to watch the event with me. Then afterwards Dan said to me, "You speak and act very similar to Bob Jones in your delivery." I took this as a compliment as Bob is a unique individual who experiences mystical encounters which are beyond most people's comprehension. Dan noticed my karate uniform sticking out of the suitcase and asked about it. I mentioned that for some time now, I had hoped to train in a martial arts school in Korea. This also led to me telling Dan about the word I received when I was a 15-year old: "Tibet and the Himalayas will be your training grounds."

Dan asked me when was my last belt promotion which I got my first black belt in 1982. The next promotion was 4th degree around the year 2000. I have to go back to North Carolina to receive my 5th degree Shihan belt promotion as this is where my instructor Butch Velez III lives. I had been putting it off for the last few years. Dan looked at me and said: "The karate promotion and prophesy are all tied together. Go for your promotion. It is all tied together."

We headed back for the next session which was a practicum. Here I was given the reverence of sharing on the Father's heart and the four keys to hearing His heart and walking in His grace and mercy.

The next day's practicum was a manifestation-filled day. As I was giving testimonies of how the seer ability affects others, my language switched automatically. I was no longer speaking English but in tongues, prayer language. Since I could not change the language, I continued with tongues. When all was finished and I could not speak at all as the Holy Spirit was in control, Dan came up, and I gave him the microphone, still not having the ability to speak English. Then Dr. Huang came up and asked, "Who wants impartation?" Everyone stood up.

The evening session started after dinner. As Dan was speaking, the Holy Spirit came again as rivers flowed inward and outward releasing greater manifestations of laughter and joy. Dan could not speak because of the laughter that overwhelmed so he threw his teaching notes into the air! The professor who was translating was getting infuriated, but then the joy of the Lord manifested in him, and he fell to the floor in laughter as the river of God flowed into healings. The week came to an end, and I began to make plans for getting my 5th degree black belt that coming May.

AFGHANISTAN

Having just got back from South Korea, I received a phone call from Jeff, a missionary I had been talking to at Bethel leader conferences. He takes teams in and out of Afghanistan on missions. He was informing me about a trip in March and wanted to know if I would be interested in going. I had been trying to connect with him for the last two years. I had no money for this journey, but my spirit ached to go. Out of faith, I got a visa for the trip. I looked for donations and ways to raise the funds to go. I took the rent money from one of my rentals and used it to buy the airline ticket. I don't like to ask for donations, but I will take them if given. This was not a wise business decision, but I knew I had to go thinking, *"If I had to get tires for my car, if they were bald, I would figure out a way."* In a sense, I robbed Peter to pay Paul. Or was I like the merchant in Matthew 13 who found a great pearl and sold all he had to obtain it[64]?

I flew in to Afghanistan two days ahead of the team, connecting in Dubai. Due to the safety of the people who are still there, I will keep this short and brief. My eyes where opened more as I was seeing in multiple dimensions at the same time from the moment I landed in Dubai. Along the drive to the facility where we stayed, I was telling the folks who picked me up what I saw taking place in the past, present, and future realms in the hills in the direction we drove. I saw in the terrain far from the road hidden encampments. Then as Jeff burst out, "I told you he's a seer! See how he knows what is going on in the surrounding hills and areas even though he has never been here to know anything."

We arrived at the compound at afternoon tea-time. I heard a loudspeaker and horn-type sound. The host announced that there is a Mosque a few blocks away and we will be hearing the horn and loudspeaker frequently.

After getting settled into the guest room shared with another, I returned to the dining room and joined everyone in conversation. It was during that time I felt led to tell the host and people who were visiting from other countries about a vision I had received

---

64 "Again, the kingdom of heaven is like a merchant in search of fine pearls, who, on finding one pearl of great value, went and sold all that he had and bought it. (Matthew 13:45-46)

back in 2005 on a Brazil mission trip.[65] Then I went into great details: leading others into the forest from the road we were on, coming out of the woods, seeing what looked like a soccer field with a home a few yards from the end of the field.

As I was describing this, one couple kept looking at each other. Then I began to describe the people in my vision as well as what they were doing. The more I told the story, the more they looked at each other in amazement. When I had finished telling of the vision, a youth who had been listening outside the door walked into the room announcing to everyone, "That is my grandparent's home!" Then the couple asked me what else I felt to release. They had asked me why I had come to Afghanistan. I told them about the word I had from God about Tibet and the Himalayas, and how that would be my training ground. I stated I hoped to find a connection for going into Tibet. Everyone wanted to know why going to Tibet would be important. "I have no idea," I replied. "I use to think it was about martial arts, but I realize now that is only the tip of the iceberg."

It was later that night the boy's father came up to me, handed me a piece of paper with a name and email address on it. He said to me, "I have a contact for you in Tibet. This name was given to me and I have held on to it for the last two to three years waiting for the person I am supposed to give this to. I do not know the contact, but I am to giving you the contact information." He told me that he would like to go up into the mountains of Tibet himself one day to pray, and then he blessed me with, "Godspeed."

This stepping stone was a marker and heading to a destination just as my experience in Brazil was. Morning came, and I was juiced, having gotten another course correction closer to the prophecy destination.

---

65 See Chapter 12.

A Prophecy and Promise

BOLDNESS

I would awaken out of periods of sleep in prayer. Being unable to sleep much, I decided to get up and go for a run as the morning sun was just beginning to break up the night. To be culturally acceptable, I had to be fully clothed with no skin showing to go running in Afghanistan. I was about to take off from a starting point when I heard, "Jericho march."

I asked, "How?" since my time was shorter than seven days.

In response, I heard, "Any way you like."

I did the running march over the next three mornings. First morning was one lap, then second day two laps, third morning four laps, seven times around. The distance I had decided to run included a Mosque and garden grounds and an area spanning about a mile. That next morning, I went onto the mosque garden grounds. I had brought my Bible and a book to read. I sat on a bench in the garden grounds reading the Bible along with releasing prayers in tongues aloud but softly. Then as I was reading, an older man came up to me speaking. I replied in tongues and shrugged my shoulders as the man continued speaking. As the man was turning to leave, he asked, "English?" I smiled and nodded my head "Yes." Then he left, and I was in some fear.

I said a moment later, "Lord, I missed a chance to connect. I pray that You, Lord, will expand by boldness just as you did for those in Acts 4. I will not let You down in Thy name, Amen." I fasted the rest of that day and until the next day at 6:00 PM. Remember Dad has a good sense of humor in fulfilling His word.

That morning I went on a 5-mile walk with others who were staying there at the compound. A native boy about 8 years old came up to me as we were walking, grabbed my hand and talked to me. I replied in tongues as we walked. We continued in this way until we parted company. In the early evening, I was getting restless. So, grabbing my Bible and book, I left the compound and headed back to the garden grounds of the mosque. I was intrigued by this book, *Life Story of E. W. Kenyon,* which told various revelations of how God worked in this man's life.

As I was reading, the little boy who had walked with me earlier that morning came up and sat next to me under the tree. I put the book up and started reading from the Bible to him as he listened. I started reading, pausing now and then to pray. I was reading to him in tongues as I could not speak Arabic. The boy seemed in such peace while listening. I wondered what the Lord was saying to the boy through me. The boy had to leave, so I put down the Bible and was looking to see—to hear—what the Holy Spirit was saying about the boy.[66]

I noticed the boy's clothes were worn out and too small on him. Maybe those were his play clothes maybe not. I knew then it was time to invest in this boy spiritually and monetarily, remembering 1 John 3:17-18:

> *But if anyone has the world's goods and sees his brother in need, yet closes his heart against him, how does God's love abide in him? Little children, let us not love in word or talk but in deed and in truth.*

Reaching into my pocket, I pulled out some money that would amount to a week's wages in that country. Having peace in my spirit, I put the cash in the boy's hands before he left. He turned to leave and then turned back to wave goodbye. I heard: *"This boy will change nations. He will do great things."*

I wrote the boy's name in the back of my Bible with the date to be a memory of the goodness of God and a remembrance for prophetic proclamation.

BROTHERS

A little later, two young men between the ages of 17-26 stopped where I was walking back and forth in prayer. They spoke to me

---

66 *"As I looked to see what the LORD is saying or will say."* (Habakkuk 2:1)

in broken English and seemed excited to practice their English with small talk. We continued talking as the group grew to about 16 young men. Then a couple of them asked me if I was Muslim. "No, I am not Muslim."

They then asked what do I believe.

"I believed in Jesus who is the Son of God," I answered.

While observing the group in the natural, my eyes opened to see into the mystical realm, showing me who the radicals were. They had like a volcano with steam pouring out over the top of their heads as I watched. I uttered under my breath, "Lord, help." Their next question came, "Why are you here"?

"To read and relax, like the rest of my brothers are doing here," I responded calmly. Then one of those with the red and white steam pouring out said, "You are not my brother if you are not Muslim!"

"Are we not all seeds of Abraham? So then, you are my brothers!"[67] I responded.

At this point, I reached over, grabbed the one who had the image of a steamy volcano just starting to show, and hugged the young man. The volcano disappeared instantly, and the expression on his face also completely changed. There was a peace that came over him as well as most of the others watching, except for the four that I call "radicals." I watched as the barriers of hate began to melt like ice and changed into running water. They looked at each other in astonishment over what had just happened with my hug. There were about eight young men who left while the others hung around after the hug. Those who were left continued to ask me questions. One asked me, "Did you go to a university?" Another asked, "How did you learn about the Bible?"

"Yes, I went to college!" There were four young men who still had a "volcano" and were making their way around me. One continued questioning me while another one started calling me "infidel."

---

67 Genesis 21.

Then I felt this presence that resided in the atmosphere. I considered the odds I was up against in this group of young men—ten to one. As I took a half step to my left, keeping the radicals in my peripheral vision, I almost collapsed suddenly as I moved into an unseen sphere. I touched something and felt its overwhelming power. I felt myself being straightened up and strengthened as I stood there answering their probing questions and gathering up my belongings to leave.

The most radical of the young men had a huge volcano erupting over and through him. He pointed to a picture I had on my Bible book cover, asking me "Who is in the picture?"

"My family…these are my sons, and that is my wife." That brief connection did something to reduce the eruptions from the young man who was now surrounded by twelve people. With the strengthening I had just received, it didn't matter how many were in the group. With that touch there came such a peace along with a profound love for all of them. I saw the ignorance in their mindsets that needed to be touched as only Jesus could do. Then one young man who was about 24 and spoke very good English said, "Let's take a walk." I was a little hesitant at first, but then agreed as I knew the Lord was with me. The four radicals stirred again as their steam increased, and I kept a constant watch. The rest of them left to go about their business.

The two of us went walking through the garden grounds and had a nice conversation. I noticed that we were being followed at a distance by the radicals. We stopped to sit on the grass on the other side of the mosque as we were enjoying one another's company. Then the leader of radicals, the one with erupting volcano, came up with two others. The young man with me excused himself and stood to intervene between me and the radical. In less than a minute, things started getting loud and fiercely intense. I knew it was time for me to go! As I stood up scanning the surroundings, I saw two men running toward us to intervene. There was a beam of heavenly light shining over both of them. As they approached, they looked at me and pointed to the exit gate, and I knew it was my queue to leave.

Upon leaving, I prayed for my new friend's protection as well as for the others who had been touched by Jesus. I prayed they would come to know the Son of God who is the Truth and the Light. My time in Afghanistan was over the next day, and I knew my friend had a good calling to walk in. Dad humor is awesome when you ask for a second chance. Sometimes I am even glad I missed or messed up the first opportunity.

Finding this key of the Father's declaration in a part of the world that has no connection in the natural brings a new understanding that we are all welcomed into God's kingdom through Jesus Christ. I loved this adventure so much I wanted to stay and be involved in some of the country games and sports. It took me a year to catch up on replenishing Peter funds—or should I say gathering cash to go after another pearl?[68] But, it was well worth it, and this pearl is beyond measure. As we continue looking for the next beacon.

SHIHAN, MORAVIAN FALLS, AND MORNINGSTAR

Lorrie felt the need to check the internet one more time for any events going on in North Carolina before buying the airline tickets. We just had a feeling something was supposed to be going on at Morningstar. The Morningstar Ministry website revealed they had just made a last minute decisssion to hold a Worship & Warfare Conference! The last one was held twenty years ago! We decided to go ahead and purchased the tickets. Flying into Charlotte, North Carolina, we rented a car and drove to Jacksonville where we met up with Butch. I spent the next two days receiving a teachers-teacher knowledge in becoming a *Shihan* in American Goshin Budo and Kobudo under Shi-Toh-Ryu Karate and Ju-Jit-Su. We also decided to spend a few days in Moravian Falls before the conference.

---

68   Matthew 13:45-46.

Upon arriving at Morivian Falls, we were put up in Rick Joyner's retreat cabin, the founder of Morningstar, and stayed there for two days. It was located on top of one of the mountains. It was a place where supernatural encounters and heavenly presence brought almost a continous open vision and revelation. If you have not been to Morivan Falls, I recommend looking up the history and making it a place to visit. With such peace and open heavens in this place, it was hard to even leave for the conference.

At this conference, I meet a young man who had a similar physical encounter as a child with being thrown around by unclean spirits. Sitting down to have lunch together, we shared our experiences. This man's run-in with unclean spirits had almost cost him his life. This conference was more than we asked for. Following that, we headed back to California.

In closing, the chronicles of this ro'eh/seer are continuing towards the Father's declaration as I follow the beacons and markers that are given. Along the journey, we learn of things about ourselves often through the choices we make on the path we choose. We have to keep checking our hearts. Life's pulls and offerings may help or hamper each of us as they bring forth desires that can tempt us for good or evil. It is the temptation that can turn desire to lust bringing issues and conflicts in truth, integrity, love, peace, and joy. Remember this, I have found it is our hearts that release power and authority naturally in gifting or abilities which can stir the Holy Spirit when it seems He is not moving.

We—this generation of all ages—are in the harvest fields now, both in life and in the harvest field of souls. Our gifts and abilities are for bringing forth the laborers in both harvest fields so that everyone gifted with a touch can become a laborer.[69] We are the

---

[69] "The harvest is plentiful, but the laborers are few; therefore pray earnestly to the Lord of the harvest to send out laborers into his harvest." (Matthew 9:37-38); I want you to think about how all this makes you more significant, not less. A body isn't just a single part blown up into something huge. It's all the

A Prophecy and Promise

Special Forces of God—each of us working together. One is in communication, another is infantry, others are doctors,[70] etc., but we are one great army, and the Holy Spirit is the Supreme Power residing in each of us. I tell you now the gifts become more alive as we walk onto the battlefield no matter where it is.

I would like to leave you with this quote from the twenty-sixth president of the United States of America.

Teddy Roosevelt once said:

It is not the critic who counts, not the man who points out how the strong man stumbles, or where the doer of deeds could have done better. The credit belongs to the man in the arena, whose face is marred by dust and sweat and blood, who strives valiantly... who knows the great enthusiasm, the great devotions; who spends himself in a worthy cause; who at the best knows in the end the triumph of high achievement, and who at the worst, if he fails, at least fails while daring greatly, so that his place shall never be with those cold and timid souls who have never know victory nor defeat.

---

different- but- similar parts arranged and functioning together. (1 Corinthians 12:14)

70 "But only God who gives the growth. He who plants and he who waters are one, and each will receive his wages according to his labor." (1Corinthians 3:5. 7)

APPENDIX I
PROPHETIC TERMS AND REFERENCES

GREEK;
Seer: ha#r* **ra'eh** (raw-eh'); from; seeing, i.e. experiencing:
ro'eh (ro-eh'); active participle of; a seer (as often rendered); but also (abstractly) a vision:
chozeh (kho-zeh'); active participle of; a beholder in vision; also a compact (as looked upon with approval): *KJV* - agreement, prophet, see that, seer, [star-] gazer.
chazowth (khaw-zooth'); from; a revelation:
Prophet: **nabiy'** (naw-bee'); from; a prophet or (generally) inspired man: *KJV* - prophecy, that prophesy, prophet.
nebiy'ah (neb-ee-yaw'); feminine of; a prophetess or (generally) inspired woman; by implication, a poetess; by association a prophet's wife:

HEBREW:
Seer – ha-ro'eh **ro'eh** (ro-eh'); active participle of; a seer (as often rendered); but also (abstractly) a vision:
Prophet – Lanaabiy **"nabiy'"** (naw-bee'); from; a prophet or (generally) inspired man:
regel (reh'-gel); a foot (as used in walking); by implication, a step; *KJV* - be able to endure, according as, after, coming, follow, journey.

ARABIC WORD MEANINGS:

Peace be upon you - Assalamu alaikum
Reply: Walaikum assalam
...and mercy - wa rahmatullahi
...and blessings - wa barakatuhu
Please - *(m):* Min fadlak, *(f):* Min fadlik

REFERENCES

The Seer by Jim W. Goll Destiny Image, Publishers, Inc. 2004 page 26, "The Seer" by Jim W. Goll, Destiny Image Publishers, Inc. 2004, www.destinyimage.com
Bob Jones, at MorningStar Ministries Charlotte, NC www.eaglestar.org
Bibliography: Mitchell, Gen. William. "Building a Futile Navy", Atlantic Monthly, September 1928
GOD'S Generals http://www.godsgenerals.com/, Biography W. Branham www.williambranham.com
Angelic encounters www.garyoates.com
John G Lake; is another who carried a supernatural calling a rich businessman from Chicago. It is recorded that scientist had put a live virus into the palm of John hands that was fatal to people, killing thousands as the virus itself died.
John & Carol Arnott along with **Randy Clark** has invited the *HOLY SPIRIT* as revival has continued since 1994 known as the "*Toronto Blessing*". www.tacf.org
Bill Johnson and *Kris Vallotton* men of vision releasing what the *Holy Spirit* requires of them globally. Kris is known seer in the prophetic realm. www.ibethel.org
Book of Daniel 10:12-14[71]

---

[71] Then he said to me, "Fear not, Daniel, for from the first day that you set your heart to understand and humbled yourself before your God, your words have been heard, and I have come because of your words. The prince of the kingdom of Persia withstood me twenty-one days, but Michael, one of the chief princes, came to help me, for I was left there with the kings of Persia, and came to make you understand what is to happen to your people in the latter days. For the vision is for days yet to come."

Warner Books; The Founding Fathers on Leadership by Donald T Phillips.
Phrases; www.sudairy.com/arabic/phrases.html
Bible, Crossway Bibles English Standard Version Classic Thinline Edition 2002
(Biblesoft's. New Exhaustive Strong's Numbers and Concordance with Expanded Greek-Hebrew Dictionary. Copyright © 1994, 2003, 2006 - Biblesoft, Inc and International Bible Translators, Inc.)
Randy Clark and his Team www.Globalawakening.com
Bill and Carol Dew http://www.dewnamis.com

REFERENCES - CHAPTER 1

Marie Curie; Smithsonian Oct 2011 www.smithsonian.com
History of infrared science: The discovery of infrared radiation is ascribed to William Herschel, the astronomer, in the early 19th century.
Other important dates include:

- 1860: Gustav Kirchhoff formulates the blackbody theorem $E=J(T,n)$;
- 1901: Max Planck published the blackbody equation and theorem. He solved the problem by quantizing the allowable energy transitions.
- Early 1900s: Albert Einstein develops the theory of the photoelectric effect, determining the photon. Also William Coblentz in spectroscopy and radiometry.
- 1917: Theodore Case develops thallous sulfide detector; British develop the first infra-red search and track (IRST) in World War I and detect aircraft at a range of one mile (1.6 km);
- 1965: First IR Handbook; first commercial imagers (Barnes, Agema {now part of FLIR Systems Inc.}; Richard Hudson's
- Visible Light Spectrum & Lasers By Andrew Zimmerman Jones, www.About.com Guide http://physics.about.com/od/lightoptics/a/vislightspec.htm

Ultra Violet; Portion of the electromagnetic spectrum extending from the violet end of visible light to the X-ray region.
The American Heritage® Science Dictionary, Copyright © 2002. Published by Houghton Mifflin. All rights reserved

Made in the USA
San Bernardino, CA
08 July 2014